W9-API-227

The LOUISIANA PURCHASE

JEFFERSON'S NOBLE BARGAIN?

The LOUISIANA PURCHASE

JEFFERSON'S NOBLE BARGAIN?

by James E. Lewis, Jr.

Preface by Lawrence S. Kaplan

THOMAS JEFFERSON FOUNDATION

Monticello Monograph Series

2003

Library of Congress Cataloging-in-Publication Data

Lewis, James E., 1964-
    The Louisiana Purchase : Jefferson's noble bargain? / James E. Lewis,
Jr. ; preface by Lawrence S. Kaplan.
        p. cm. -- (Monticello monograph series)
Includes bibliographical references and index.
    ISBN 1-882886-23-2 (alk. paper)
    1. Louisiana Purchase. 2. Jefferson, Thomas, 1743-1826. I. Title.
II. Series.
E333 .L63 2003
973.4'6--dc22

                                                            2003016947

ON THE COVER

Napoleon Crossing the Alps by school of Jacques-Louis David (early 19th century; courtesy of the Louisiana State Museum) and the velvet silk cover of the French exchange copy of one of the conventions that comprise the Louisiana Purchase (National Archives). In background, signatures of Thomas Jefferson and Napoleon Bonaparte. Bonaparte's is taken from the above convention (National Archives).

Copyright © 2003 by Thomas Jefferson Foundation, Inc.

Designed by Gibson Design Associates.
Edited and coordinated by Beth L. Cheuk.

This book was made possible by support from the
Martin S. and Luella Davis Publications Endowment.

Distributed by
The University of North Carolina Press
Chapel Hill, North Carolina 27515-2288
1-800-848-6224

This book may not be reproduced in whole or in part in any form or by any means, electronic or mechanical, including photocopying, recording, or by any information storage and retrieval system now known or hereafter invented, without written permission from the publisher.

THOMAS JEFFERSON FOUNDATION, INC.

TRUSTEES

Thomas A. Saunders III
Chairman

Rebecca W. Rimel
Vice Chairman

Hunter J. Smith
Secretary

Jeffrey C. Walker
Treasurer

Michael R. Beschloss
J. Stewart Bryan III
Alfonso L. Carney, Jr.
Adele Chatfield-Taylor
John F. Cooke
Mrs. Martin S. Davis
B. Grady Durham
Albert D. Ernest, Jr.
Richard Gilder
John A. Griffin
Alice W. Handy
R. Crosby Kemper III

EMERITUS TRUSTEES
Mrs. George M. Cochran
Brenton S. Halsey

HONORARY TRUSTEES
Francis L. Berkeley
Wendell D. Garrett
R. Crosby Kemper
David McCullough
Merrill D. Peterson

PRESIDENT
Daniel P. Jordan

CONTENTS

*Thomas Jefferson (1804) by Charles Fevret de
Saint-Mémin. (Thomas Jefferson Foundation, Inc.)*

PREFACE

Among the many grievances that Alexander Hamilton nourished against Thomas Jefferson was the acquisition of New Orleans from France, an objective that Hamilton himself had long wanted. He believed that the president lacked the nerve to take on France. When Jefferson won Louisiana without war or new sources of revenue, Hamilton admitted grudgingly that Jefferson had won an impressive diplomatic victory. But he attributed his success "solely … to a fortuitous concurrence of unforeseen and unexpected circumstances, and not to any wise or vigorous measures on the part of the American government." In other words, Jefferson was a beneficiary of just plain luck.

The Louisiana Purchase consisted of more than luck. In his lucid examination of this achievement, James E. Lewis, Jr., has illuminated the problems attending the politics and diplomacy of the purchase with particular insight into Jefferson's hopes and fears. Much of the story is familiar: Napoleon's secret purchase from Spain, British disclosure of the action, the president's use of Du Pont de Nemours to signal American needs, the dispatch of Monroe to help Livingston, and the surprise offer of all Louisiana to the two diplomats. Lewis enriches this account with nuanced interpretations of some of the more controversial elements in the negotiating process.

When Jefferson ominously observed in his private letter to Livingston that if France takes possession of New Orleans, "we must marry ourselves to the British fleet and nation," it was intended as a ploy to influence Bonaparte. Livingston had been urging Rufus King in London to enlist British support surreptitiously without letting France know of this effort. What bothered Jefferson and Madison, as Lewis points out, was the potential embarrassment if Livingston's clandestine activities became known to the French. They were concerned that Britain might indeed participate in attempts to thwart French plans, but at a price that the United States would find unacceptable. Jefferson's "private" letter "invoked" Britain without compromising any American options. He wanted to gain the benefits of a British connection without "paying any of the costs" of British involvement. Lewis's gloss on the matter makes it clear that Jefferson had not changed his mind about the British menace. A British Louisiana was even less acceptable than a French Louisiana. A French settlement west of the Mississippi inevitably would be weaker than the British neighbor in Canada moving into Upper Louisiana, north of the Missouri River.

Lewis untangles the seemingly confusing approaches Jefferson took to the territories west of the Mississippi. One of them was to distance himself from the idea of acquiring all of Spanish Louisiana. New Orleans and Florida had been the goals of Livingston and Monroe in Paris. Beyond New Orleans, the territory east of the Mississippi would respond to demands of westerners to secure control of traffic on the river. The lands west of the river were another matter, and one that plagued the Jeffersonians almost as much as it did the Federalists. While worries about the political affiliations of westerners and about the attractiveness of the West were reasons for Federalist opposition, the Jeffersonians could welcome such outcomes and still have qualms about the ramifications of expansion beyond the Mississippi. It was not that the administration refused to think about the West. Jefferson had been intrigued for years by the possibilities of an "empire of liberty" that would embrace the continent. His encouragement of George Rogers Clark's campaigns during the Revolution and of John Ledyard's proposed explorations after the war as well as his sponsorship of the Lewis and Clark Expedition during his presidency revealed the extent of his aspirations.

But in 1803 they were countered by more immediate dangers that could arise from actual possession of these territories. Most historians have concentrated on Jefferson's fears of a French Louisiana that would block American expansion, or on worries about the feasibility of a constitutional amendment. Lewis notes that these were not the critical issues. Rather, it was the stability of the United States itself that might be at stake through the creation of one or more independent states from unchecked immigration to the Louisiana territories. Alternatively, should France retain New Orleans, Bonaparte might tempt westerners to secede from the Union more effectively than Spain had done in the 1780s. The image of bellicose settlers of uncertain loyalty to the Union made Jeffersonians uneasy about the acquisition of all Louisiana.

Repeatedly, Lewis raises the image of "neighborhood" as both a promise and a threat. At one point Jefferson was hopeful that even if westerners separated from the Union, they would still be Americans sharing as neighbors the values of the United States. His more abiding prediction was that restless westerners would not necessarily be good neighbors. The author seems to have in mind "the problem of neighborhood" that he dealt with so effectively in his *The American Union and the Problem of Neighborhood: The United States and the Collapse of the Spanish Empire, 1783-1829.* Conflict rather than harmony might be the consequence of new communities inside the Louisiana territories but outside the Union's control. A separate federation could become a dangerous neighbor.

The president postulated scenarios that would take care of both the Indian and the territorial problems. By removing Indians from the east to the west side of the Mississippi, he could use them as a police force to prevent white settlements. Jefferson assumed that this arrangement would keep Americans in the trans-Appalachian West until those lands were filled. Only then would orderly settlement be encouraged, at which time the Indians would be moved further West. This plan was no more practical than his hope of keeping slavery out of the Louisiana territories. Inevitably, it was abandoned as he faced the possibility of Bonaparte changing his mind. James Lewis concludes his insightful study with a recognition that the problems of settlement, of governance, and of territorial boundaries were ultimately managed without disruption of the Union. The one major issue that was not resolved—slavery in the Louisiana territories—provides a case study of luck running out.

— Lawrence S. Kaplan
Georgetown University

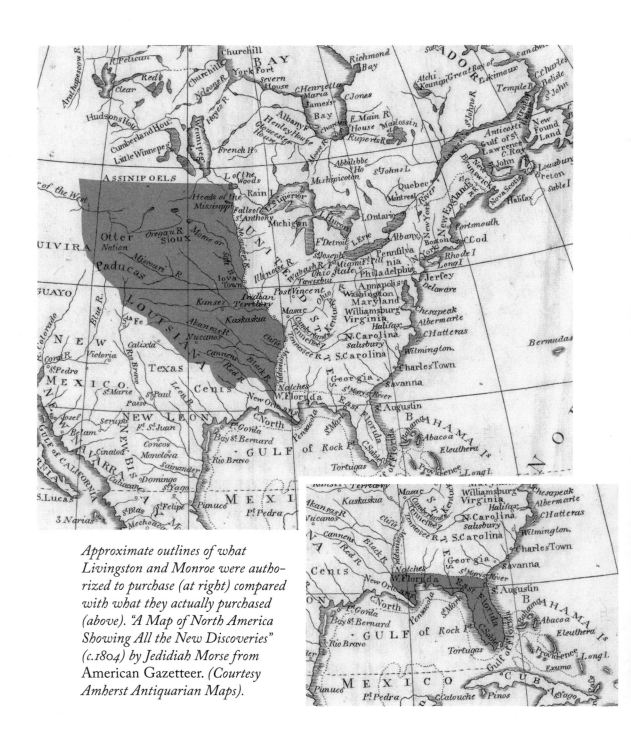

Approximate outlines of what Livingston and Monroe were authorized to purchase (at right) compared with what they actually purchased (above). "A Map of North America Showing All the New Discoveries" (c.1804) by Jedidiah Morse from American Gazetteer. *(Courtesy Amherst Antiquarian Maps).*

Chapter One

WASHINGTON, JULY 1803

On the evening of July 3, 1803, the eve of the anniversary of American independence, President Thomas Jefferson received the stunning news that the United States had purchased "the island of N[ew] Orleans and all Louisiana" from France. On April 30, the administration's representatives in Paris, Robert R. Livingston and James Monroe, had signed a treaty with Napoleon Bonaparte's minister of finance, François Barbé-Marbois. The first reports of the treaty that reached Washington did not include its precise terms. What were Louisiana's boundaries? How much had Livingston and Monroe agreed to pay for it? What conditions had been attached to the sale? But Jefferson believed that the purchased territory was "something larger than the whole US." Confidently, he informed his son-in-law that the new acquisition "removes from us the greatest source of danger to our peace."[1]

What was stunning to the president was not that Livingston and Monroe had succeeded in removing the "danger to our peace," though there had certainly been ample reason to doubt whether their negotiations would succeed, but that they had done so by purchasing "all Louisiana." For more than two years, Jefferson and his cabinet—Secretary of State James Madison, Secretary of the Treasury Albert Gallatin, Secretary of War Henry Dearborn, Secretary of the Navy Robert Smith, and Attorney General Levi Lincoln—had worried about the short- and long-term implications of France's recovery of the immense province of Louisiana from Spain. They had considered and proposed numerous ways to resolve this delicate situation. But at no time before Livingston and Monroe concluded the treaty had Jefferson or Madison suggested, or authorized, purchasing all of Louisiana. In fact, Madison's instructions had never discussed purchasing any territory

Thomas Jefferson (1789) by Jean-Antoine Houdon. (Thomas Jefferson Foundation, Inc.)

west of the Mississippi River. What the administration actually wanted was to acquire all of the territory *east* of the river—what was then called the "island" of New Orleans and the provinces of East and West Florida—from whichever power, France or Spain, owned them. When Livingston and Monroe informed Madison of the treaty, they opened their letter by acknowledging that "an acquisition of so great an extent was, we well Know, not contemplated by our appointment." In a private letter to his friend the secretary of state, Monroe admitted that if they could "have procur'd a part of the territory we shod. never have thot. of getting the whole." To ease the two ministers' minds, the cabinet decided in mid-July to send them a letter "expressly approving [of] their obtaining Louisiana."[2]

It is not that Jefferson and his cabinet had never imagined expansion beyond the Mississippi. By July 1803, Americans had been thinking about westward expansion for nearly twenty years, beginning not long after the Treaty of Paris (1783) ended the Revolutionary War and established the Mississippi as the western boundary of the United States. Madison had not included "the purchase of the *country beyond the Mississippi*" in the official instructions sent to Livingston and Monroe because it "was *not deemd* at this *time within* the *pale of probability.*" In the spring of 1803, the acquisition of territory west of the river was not just seen as improbable, however; it was also considered unnecessary. Jefferson and Madison believed that they could resolve the crisis created by France's return to Louisiana after nearly four decades of Spanish rule without expanding beyond the river. They certainly did not oppose westward expansion; but their ideas about it were not nearly as simple as their ultimate accomplishments might lead us to expect. Over the preceding two decades, as they had thought about first the region between the Appalachian Mountains and the Mississippi and later the immense continent beyond the river, their dreams, and even expectations, of expansion had almost always been balanced with concerns, and even fears, about its results. (Much of the official correspondence was in code; italicized words generally indicate decoded passages, as noted in the endnotes.)[3]

These concerns did not immediately disappear with the news of the Louisiana Purchase. Jefferson's political opponents, the Federalists, immediately began criticizing the treaty. Some considered it the fortuitous outcome of a bad policy. Some objected to the expense. Some evinced what Madison described as a "spirit of indiscriminate *objection to public measures.*" But most Federalists criticized the treaty precisely because of its principal feature, the acquisition of a vast field for expansion beyond the Mississippi. It was not only the Federalists who expressed this concern.

Napoleon Bonaparte (after 1807), copy after Antoine Denis Chaudet. (Thomas Jefferson Foundation, Inc.)

One of the first responses of many Republicans, including Monroe and Jefferson, was to try to find some means for preventing Americans from moving across the river. "Perhaps the best course," Monroe noted just two weeks after agreeing to spend millions to purchase Louisiana, would "be to keep it for many years vacant." Within just two days of learning of the treaty, Jefferson had already devised a plan that he believed would close the vast majority of Louisiana to white settlement "for half a century" or more.[4]

Certainly, most Americans—including Jefferson, Monroe, and even many Federalists—saw the Louisiana Purchase as a "very happy acquisition." But it was not unproblematic, either in July 1803 or later. Caspar Wistar, the Philadelphia scientist who helped prepare Meriwether Lewis for his famous expedition, suggested the potential of the purchase in a mid-July letter of congratulations to Jefferson. He viewed the purchase "as the most important & beneficial transaction which has occurred Since the declaration of Independence, & next to it, most like[ly] to influence or regulate the destinies of our Country." Wistar was, in some respects, more correct than he could have known. Like the Declaration of Independence, the Louisiana Purchase forced Americans to reexamine some fundamental questions about their polity and society—questions about governance, slavery, union, and the young nation's place in the world. Aware of its transformative potential, Americans viewed the purchase with a mix of excitement and trepidation.[5]

Chapter Two

'ON THIS ATTACHMENT DEPENDS OUR HAPPINESS'

How Americans reacted to Louisiana's "retrocession" (as it was formally known) from Spain to France in 1800 and its sale by France to the United States in 1803 reflected an understanding of the United States and its North American neighborhood that had developed during the preceding quarter century. The same mix of hope and fear that characterized their response to the Louisiana Purchase had been apparent for years in their thinking about the West, whether the trans-Appalachian West between the mountains and the river or the trans-Mississippi West beyond. Perceiving themselves as a dynamic, growing people, they had long imagined themselves displacing the current Native American and Spanish occupants, whom they viewed as stagnant and declining. But how would Americans west of the mountains, or the river, interact with those along the Atlantic coast?

Even before 1776, Americans had looked beyond the mountains expectantly and had denounced and defied British efforts to keep them east of the Appalachians. For many, independence from Great Britain meant a prospect of new lands and new opportunities in the West. Actually acquiring these lands and making good on these opportunities was a different story, as the native peoples of the trans-Appalachian West continued to resist the American advance long after their British ally gave up the fight. Despite their inability to take control of the trans-Appalachian West, some Americans began to cast their eyes beyond the Mississippi soon after the war ended. Even before the end of the 1780s, Jedidiah Morse, the author of *The American Geography: or A View of the Present Situation of the United States of America*, could already "anticipate the period, as not far distant, when the AMERICAN EMPIRE will comprehend millions of souls, west of the Mississippi."[6]

Jefferson certainly shared this expectation that Americans would expand beyond the Mississippi boundary. In a fascinating letter from January 1786, he insisted that "our confederacy must be viewed as the nest from which all America, North and South is to be peopled." It was not that Jefferson believed that the rest of the New World was empty; he reported in the same letter that a recent revolution in Spanish America had "cost on both sides an hundred thousand lives." But Spain's colonies had not seen anything like the demographic explosion of Great Britain's, where the population doubled about every twenty-two years. Jefferson returned to this idea fifteen years later. In "distant times," he predicted to Monroe, "our rapid multiplication will expand itself beyond [the nation's original] limits, and cover the whole northern, if not the southern continent, with a people speaking the same language, governed in similar forms, and by similar laws."[7]

James Madison, President of the United States of America, *engraving after 1804 portrait by Gilbert Stuart. (Thomas Jefferson Foundation, Inc.)*

But did the expansion of the American people necessarily mean the expansion of the American union? At the time, Jefferson seemed to think not. The new governments beyond the Mississippi would be republican, with "similar forms" and "similar laws," but that did not guarantee that they would be parts of the United States. Like many Americans, he believed that the New World's future governments—whether over the mountains or across the river or beyond—might possibly, even probably, emerge outside of the American union. This widely shared recognition fueled the concerns and fears that coexisted with the dreams and expectations in the thinking about American expansion.

A clear understanding of the dangers of "neighborhood," as Jefferson and his contemporaries often referred to it, developed over the course of the 1780s. The original confederation uniting the thirteen former colonies was an artifact of the

Revolutionary War. With independence assured after 1783, the primary cement of the union—the British enemy—disappeared. At the same time, the efforts to govern a young, weak, and indebted nation frequently exposed the very different interests of the various states and regions. By the mid-1780s, the founding generation found itself forced to consider the possibility that the United States would dissolve into either thirteen or more separate states or three or four partial confederacies. Europe's example taught them that sovereign nations could not coexist peacefully alongside each other. "To look for a continuation of harmony between a number of independent unconnected sovereignties, situated in the same neighbourhood," as Alexander Hamilton remarked, was "to disregard the uniform course of human events."[8]

James Monroe, President of the United States of America, *engraving by Thomas Gilbrede (1817) after portrait by John Vanderlyn. (Thomas Jefferson Foundation, Inc.)*

Understood in this way, neighborhood jeopardized the goals for which Americans had just fought—national independence and republican government. Collisions between neighbors over trade, borders, and laws were inevitable. Independent nations would have the duty to protect and advance their rights and interests using whatever means were necessary. The larger states would swallow up their smaller neighbors, as had happened in Europe. Weaker states, or confederacies, would try to defend themselves against their stronger neighbors in two ways. They would look abroad for support, sacrificing some of their independence in exchange for British, French, or Spanish protection. And they would adopt measures that seemed inconsistent with republican government—centralizing power, organizing standing armies, erecting expensive fortifications, and paying for it all with crushing taxes and forced levies. "If we should be disunited," Hamilton reasoned in *The Federalist*, "we should be in a short course of time, in the predicament of the continental powers of Europe—

our liberties would be a prey to the means of defending ourselves against the ambition and jealousy of each other."[9]

This developing understanding of the problem of neighborhood drove the movement to replace the existing confederation with the "more perfect union" of the Constitution. By transferring more of the rights and obligations of sovereignty from the states to the federal government, the new Constitution would restrict the means by which the states could promote their interests. Conflicts between the states would not disappear, but politics and law would replace war as the means to resolve them. A single union would help to exclude European interference in North American affairs. It would promote and protect republican government in the states. It would also bring prosperity, whether by creating an extensive field for unrestricted exchange within the union or by providing the economic leverage to force open new markets around the world. Finally, the new federal government would command the manpower, resources, and money needed to remove the obstacles to expansion into the trans-Appalachian West and, in time, perhaps beyond.

Robert Livingston, engraving by H.B. Hall. (Courtesy of Louisiana State Museum)

This understanding of the dangers of neighborhood emerged in the context not merely of the growing prospect of disunion in the East, but also of the ongoing problem of governance in the West. With the war against Great Britain ended, the trans-Appalachian West presented one of the most important fields for action by the confederation government. Before 1781, the entirety of the West was claimed by the various eastern states on the basis of their colonial charters. In that year, Virginia agreed to cede its claims to the region north and west of the Ohio River to the general government if the other states would cede their western claims. Virginia still included modern Kentucky (as well as West Virginia), North

Carolina still encompassed modern Tennessee, and Georgia still claimed west to the Mississippi, but the cessions made the confederation government responsible for the so-called Northwest Territory beyond the Ohio. How should this region be governed? And what should be done with Kentucky and Tennessee, whose citizens were already beginning to think that their state governments were too distant?

To many, the greatest danger was that the western settlers would establish independent governments outside the union. In 1784, George Washington, who as soldier and surveyor had extensive firsthand knowledge of the West, predicted that westerners would soon "become a distinct people from us." The western states would "have different views [and] different interests," which would invariably compete and conflict with those of the coastal states. "Instead of adding strength to the Union," Washington warned, they would become "a formidable & dangerous neighbour." During the 1780s, there were good reasons to worry as separatist movements swept across the backcountry and the West. Vermont survived as an independent nation outside the union for nearly fifteen years, from 1777 to 1791. During that time, it negotiated with British officials in Canada, fought off incursions by New York troops, and even tried to wrest territory away from New Hampshire. In the mountains of southwestern Virginia, western North Carolina, and eastern Tennessee, citizens erected the new state of Franklin. Like Vermont, Franklin hoped to join the union. To eastern leaders, its very existence, even if only temporary, suggested what western settlers might do if the state and federal governments lost control in the West.[10]

Most eastern leaders recoiled in horror from the possibility that, as Madison put it in 1785, the future states "on the waters of the Mississippi [might have] to be viewed in the same relation to the Atlantic States as exists between the heterogeneous and hostile Societies of Europe." They agreed on the importance of bringing stability to the trans-Appalachian West and attaching it to the union. But the consensus extended only to goals, not means. Some eastern leaders hoped to discourage settlement for a number of years, during which time the government could work to cement its control over the West. A variety of measures could be used to further this plan—slowing the transfer of western land from the government to actual settlers and making the process by which territories would become states a lengthy one, among others. But the most promising, in the view of many of the New York and New England members in the confederation Congress, was to accept Spain's decision to close the Mississippi to American trade for a period of twenty-five to thirty years. These men—most of whom would later become Federalists—reasoned that, once it became clear that there would be no outlet for western produce for many years, potential migrants would stay in the East.[11]

Many of the men who would later form the Republican party—including Jefferson, Madison, and Monroe—offered very different solutions to the problem of the West. They believed that East and West could be held together only by bonds of interest, not by efforts at compulsion. The confederation government needed to show an active and immediate commitment to meeting western needs, whether economic, political, or diplomatic. Westerners wanted access to land, protection from the Indians, progress toward self-government, and use of the Mississippi. And they would have these things, Jefferson and others accepted, within the union or without it. The eastern governments, whether of the states or the confederation, were simply too weak to prevent western settlement or to force western settlers to remain in a form of colonial subserviency. Unless Congress met the legitimate needs of western settlers, Jefferson predicted to Monroe in 1786, they would "end by separating from our confederacy and becoming it's enemies." Such views insured that these future Republicans would oppose the future Federalists' attempts to close the river for a generation.[12]

The struggle between these two groups reached a peak over the negotiations between John Jay and the Spanish minister, Don Diego de Gardoqui, in 1786 and 1787. In 1784, Spain closed the river to American trade on the grounds that it owned both banks of the Mississippi from the Gulf of Mexico to at least the 31st Parallel. In 1786, a coalition of northern congressmen, representing a majority of the states, pushed through Congress approval for Jay to negotiate a treaty in which the United States would forego its claim to use the river for twenty-five to thirty years in exchange for trading privileges elsewhere in Spain's empire. Westerners were outraged. Vague plans for a separation from the union and an agreement with Spain suddenly turned into more definite actions, particularly in Kentucky. A letter that Madison received from Pittsburgh in early 1787 convinced him "that by degrees the people [of the West might] be led to set up for themselves." Monroe, a member of the Virginia delegation in Congress, soon emerged as one of the firmest opponents of the negotiations, earning the lasting trust of westerners. In his thinking, accepting the closure of the river seemed so certain to end in disunion that the intent of the measure's sponsors could only have been to "[throw] the western people & territory without the Govt. of the U S." Though in the minority, the southern states had enough votes to prevent the ratification of the treaty and thwart the negotiations. But the failure of the treaty did not mean that Spain had to open the river to western trade.[13]

Although serving abroad as the American minister to France during this controversy, Jefferson received regular reports about it from Monroe and Madison. His analysis of the crisis included most of the elements of his later thinking about the return of Louisiana to France. Free use of the Mississippi was "a sine qua non [an absolute necessity] with us." We would only "deceive them"—Spain in 1786, France in 1801—"and ourselves to suppose that an amity [could] be preserved while this right is witheld." To think otherwise would require "an ignorance" not only of the interests of westerners, but also "of the nature of man." For reasons of sentiment and interest, westerners wanted "to remain united with us." Still, their *"separation"* had to be treated as *possible* at every moment." "The moment we [the East] sacrifice their interests to our own, they will see it better to govern themselves." Instead, the easterners who ran the country needed to "[make] all the just claims of our fellow citizens, wherever situated, our own." "No other conduct can attach us together," Jefferson warned; "and on this attachment depends our happiness." No one involved in this controversy was looking beyond the Mississippi at this time; yet almost all of Jefferson's later ideas were already present.[14]

Understanding what the founding generation learned about the problem of neighborhood and the solution of union over the course of the 1780s helps explain the crisis created by the retrocession of Louisiana to France in 1800. Most accounts of the events leading up to the Louisiana Purchase have missed the real fears. They have suggested that the administration's great concern was—or, at least, should have been—the threat of Napoleonic France to American security. Or they have argued that Jefferson and his cabinet worried that a French Louisiana would block American expansion beyond the Mississippi. Or they have suggested that an agrarian-minded Jefferson feared that, without the vast acreage of Louisiana, men who might have become virtuous farmers would instead be forced to live in cities and work in factories. What is clear, though, is that Jefferson, his cabinet members, and many of his contemporaries were primarily worried about the impact of French control over the Mississippi on the stability of the union. They feared that if mishandled, this crisis, like that occasioned by Spain's closure of the river in the 1780s, could end in an independent *American* nation beyond the Appalachians that would be far more destructive of the goals of the Revolution than a weak *French* colony beyond the Mississippi.

Chapter Three

WASHINGTON, SUMMER 1801

In the summer of 1801, and for many years after, Washington, D.C., presented perhaps the least imposing national capital in the world. The federal government had moved to the city just the previous year, exchanging populous and cosmopolitan Philadelphia for a place that, according to one congressman, lacked only "houses, [wine] cellars, kitchens, scholarly men, amiable women, and a few other such trifles" to make it perfect. A few clusters of private homes, public buildings, and boarding houses stood amidst the acres of forest, field, and swamp that comprised the new city. One cluster had sprung up around the still-unfinished Capitol, another around the still-unfinished Executive Mansion; but there was barely more than a cleared lane connecting them. Even at peak times of the year, when both the Supreme Court and Congress were in session, there were barely 300 federal officials and employees in the city, other than the small detachment at the Navy Yard. Most of the time, the number was closer to 150.[15]

Jefferson's inauguration in early March 1801 brought to a close an election that was as tight, bitter, and divisive as any in American history. In the end, he had to defeat both his Federalist opponent, John Adams, and his Republican "running mate," Aaron Burr, when a tie in the electoral college vote threw the decision into the House of Representatives. Jefferson's administration thus began at a time of constitutional crisis, sectional division, party rivalry, and intra-party tension. Americans needed a chance to recover—and to discover what it meant to transfer power from the ruling party to the opposition. And Jefferson's inaugural address promised real change. In it, he called for eliminating most taxes, reducing government expenses, cutting the army and navy, lowering the national debt, and avoiding foreign entanglements. But could this system of policy easily accommodate, or be accommodated to, a new crisis?

Early in Jefferson's presidency, rumors began to reach the United States of a recent, secret agreement between France and Spain concerning Louisiana. They came in newspapers, in private letters, in reports by merchants and travelers, and, in time, in official dispatches from American diplomats abroad. They arrived in Washington when Congress was in recess—the usual condition in the early decades of the new government—and not expected to be back in session until early December. And they reached Jefferson and his cabinet at a time when they were still setting up their homes and offices in the new capital city.

The earliest rumors found the State Department in a time of transition. Though nominated and confirmed in the first days of the new administration, Madison did not actually take over the management of the department until early May. At that time, the State Department had ministers (the United States did not appoint "ambassadors" until the end of the nineteenth century) in five European countries—Great Britain, Spain, Portugal, Prussia, and the Netherlands—and consuls (commercial agents) in a number of European, North African, and

The Senate Wing of the Unfinished United States Capitol, Washington, D.C. *by William R. Birch, 1800. (Library of Congress)*

Caribbean port cities. All of them were Federalist holdovers from the Adams administration; most of the ministers would soon be on their way back to the United States; and three of the missions—to the Netherlands, Portugal, and Prussia—were destined to be shut down entirely. For the present, Rufus King would stay in London. Jefferson and Madison had chosen Livingston to reopen the American mission in Paris and Charles Pinckney to go to Madrid; but they would not be able to leave for their posts until the fall.

From London, King provided the most reliable, and the most worrisome, of the early information. In a letter that arrived in Washington in late May, he related new evidence that supported the rumor that Spain had "ceded Louisiana and the Floridas to France." To King, what seemed most alarming was that "certain influential Persons in France" considered the Appalachians a natural "line of Separation between the People of the United States living upon the two sides of the ... Mountains." As such, King feared "that this cession is intended to have, and may actually produce, Effects injurious to the Union and consequent happiness of the People of the United States." Other reports from American diplomats in Europe were neither so confident nor so alarmist. The minister at The Hague still viewed the cession as doubtful in a letter that reached Madison in June. Even when he decided that it probably had taken place, he still believed that it might "[prove] rather favourable to us," by creating "a new temporary interest [in France] to be well with the U.S."[16]

That France wanted to recover Louisiana from Spain had been amply demonstrated long before the secret Treaty of San Ildefonso finally accomplished this goal in October 1800. In 1793, during Jefferson's service as secretary of state in the Washington administration, the revolutionary government of France had tried to wrest the province from Spain by force. After the restoration of the long-standing alliance between the two powers in 1795, rumors began to circulate that negotiations for the transfer of Louisiana were in progress. In the context of growing tensions between France and the United States over a variety of issues, these early rumors had certainly caused concern. In May 1797, Jefferson, who was then Adams's vice president, worried that "the exchange which is to give us new neighbors in Louisiana" would expose the United States "to combinations of enemies

[France and Spain] on that side where we are most vulnerable." Hamilton, the leading Federalist, called the expected transfer a "mighty mischief," the "magnitude" of which could not easily "be calculated." He pressed the Adams administration to march an army to the southwestern frontier and "tak[e] possession of [Louisiana and the Floridas] for ourselves." Doing so, Hamilton insisted, would "obviate the mischief of their falling into the hands of an Active foreign power" and "secure to the United States the advantage of keeping the key of the Western Country." In contrast, Jefferson, though obviously concerned, suggested little in the way of positive action.[17]

Jefferson could respond cautiously to the false rumors of the late 1790s—as he would to the actual transfer after 1800—because the situation on the Mississippi had changed dramatically since the late 1780s. In 1795, the United States and Spain had signed the Treaty of San Lorenzo, opening the river to American trade and providing for the United States a "right of deposit" in New Orleans. This treaty recognized that western Americans had the right to bring their produce down the river, even below the 31st Parallel where Spain owned both banks, to unload it to New Orleans's docks and warehouses, and to reload it from there onto ocean-going vessels. As Washington's secretary of state in 1790, Jefferson had initiated the negotiations that finally produced a treaty in 1795, long after he had resigned from office. When he drafted those instructions, he had shown a willingness to go to war with Spain, if necessary, to secure the use of the river and preserve the union with the trans-Appalachian West. But he had also suggested the limits of his expansionism by arguing in his "Outline of Policy on the Mississippi Question" that it would not be "our interest to cross the Missisipi for ages" and would "never be our interest to remain united with those who do." Often called Pinckney's Treaty (after the American negotiator, Thomas Pinckney), the Treaty of San Lorenzo could easily have been "Jefferson's Treaty." Washington had initially asked his former secretary of state to go to Madrid as "a special Envoy" in 1794. Assuring his successor in the State Department that "no circumstances ... will ever more tempt me to engage in any thing public," Jefferson turned down the offer. Nonetheless, the treaty could fairly be ascribed to the instructions that he had prepared as secretary of state. It did not accomplish all that Jefferson might have wished, but it did open the Mississippi to American trade and, thus, eased the separatist pressures in the West.[18]

With the use of the river and the right of deposit secured by the Treaty of San Lorenzo, Jefferson and Madison could react with concern, rather than alarm, when King's earliest dispatches regarding the Treaty of San Ildefonso reached Washington in late May 1801. What quickly became clear was how little they really knew. Even though news of the treaty had arrived "thro' several channels," Madison had to admit that "neither the extent of the cession ... nor the consideration on which it is made" were "reduced to certainty and precision." Equally unclear were the implications of the treaty. Madison initially thought that a "conciliating policy" on the part of France was a possibility, particularly if skillful American diplomacy could convey the importance of such an approach. But "what new turn time may give it" remained to be seen. Jefferson's initial assessment was a bit darker. Writing to Monroe a day after reading King's first letter, he noted that the cession was "very ominous to us."[19]

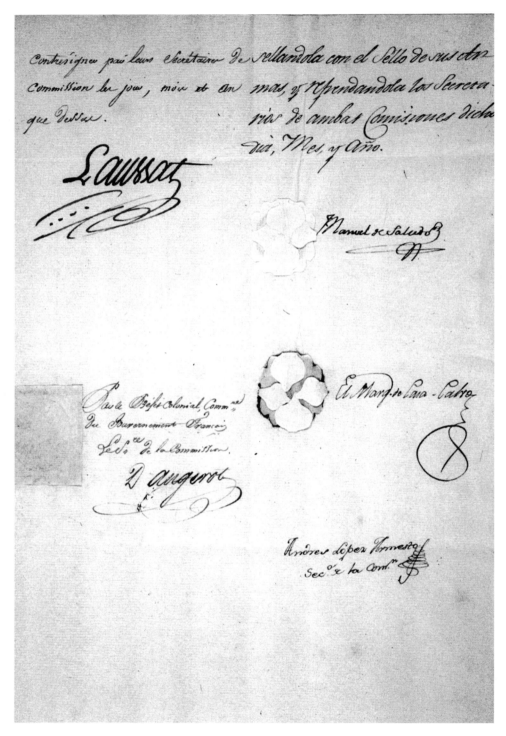

Signature page from the Proces-Verbal on the retrocession of Louisiana from Spain to France, November 30, 1803. (Courtesy Historic New Orleans Collection; MSS 125, folder 286)

Chapter Four

'TIME AND CHANGE MAY WORK IN OUR FAVOR'

In his 1786 letter to Archibald Stuart that described the United States "as the nest from which all America … [was] to be peopled," Jefferson asserted that the rest of the New World could not "be in better hands" than those of "the Spaniards." "My fear," he admitted, was "that they are too feeble to hold [it] till our population can be sufficiently advanced to gain it from them peice by peice." The news that reached Washington in early 1801 seemed to justify this fear: a "feeble" Spain had proved unable to hold Louisiana and the Floridas when faced with pressure from a strong France. One of the first things to emerge from the administration's efforts to assess the new situation was a ranking of the union's potential neighbors on its southern and western frontiers. Spain, the weakest of the likely contenders, was the most desirable. In one of the administration's earliest letters on the subject, Madison reminded Pinckney of the United States's "preference" for "the neighbourhood of Spain over that of every other nation." With its successful army, impressive navy, and vaulting ambition, Napoleonic France seemed much less desirable. But it was Great Britain, not France, that the administration considered "the last of neighbours that would be agreeable to the United States." As they shaped a response to the retrocession over the next two years, Jefferson, his advisors in Washington, and his agents abroad would always include Great Britain, along with France and Spain, in their calculations.[20]

The administration's initial response reflected both its uncertainty about the existence of a retrocession treaty and its analysis of the reasons behind France's recovery of Louisiana. To Jefferson and Madison, the treaty seemed so indefinite, so mysterious, that they could hope that it did not exist. Or, if it did exist, they could imagine France and Spain having such a weak attachment to it that they would simply abandon it if urged to by the United States. The initial instructions to Livingston, en route to Paris, and Pinckney, en route to Madrid, left no doubt that their primary charge was "to prevent a change of our Southern and South Western neighbours" by "proper means"—"that is to say the means of peace and persuasion."[21]

Discovering the best means of "persuasion" seemed to require understanding why France wanted Louisiana and the Floridas. Even without knowing exactly what the treaty included, or even whether a treaty had been concluded, Jefferson and Madison believed that they understood its source. They explained it by looking to the recent past. French interest in reacquiring Louisiana seemed the natural result of the anti-French, pro-British policies of the Adams administration. A retrocession treaty, whether already signed or only under consideration, was "properly chargeable to [the previous administration's] measures & policy." France wanted Louisiana, according to this logic, to counteract "the Atlantic States['] ... partiality for Great Britain" and to prevent "the mouth of the Mississippi" from falling into British hands, an event that would have "strengthen[ed Great Britain's] hold on the United States" and given it a commercial "monopoly of the immense and fertile region" on both sides of the river. If France sought Louisiana for these reasons, then the United States might be able to prevent the retrocession by allaying these fears. "Our conduct and our communications," Madison informed Pinckney and Livingston, had to demonstrate "that the Atlantic States [were] not disposed to enter, nor [were] in danger of being drawn into[,] partialities towards Great Britain" and that the United States, "so long as they are guided by the clearest policy," could never favor British acquisition of "any part of the Spanish possessions on the Mississippi." At its most basic level, this approach relied upon convincing France that the new, Republican administration would never act as the old, Federalist one had.[22]

On another level, however, Jefferson and Madison tried to warn France that its return to Louisiana would breed unnecessary tensions with an otherwise friendly United States. Madison's first instructions to Livingston and Pinckney provided a list of considerations "to be employed on the occasion." There was "the danger to which the Western settlements of the United States would be subject[ed] … by military expeditions between [British] Canada and [French] Louisiana." There was "the inquietude which would be excited in the Southern States, whose numerous slaves ha[d] been taught to regard the French as the patrons of their cause." But, most importantly, there was the general problem of neighborhood. However much the United States, under a Republican administration, wanted "to maintain harmony and confidence with" France, the very fact of neighborhood would produce friction and conflict. Just "the contact of their territories," Madison explained, would create a "danger of collisions between the two Republics." Trying to regulate jointly the commerce of the Mississippi guaranteed additional conflicts. Madison even suggested that, in time, France might discover that its return to Louisiana had precisely the opposite effect than that intended, as the "jealousies and apprehensions" fueled by "a French neighbourhood" might "turn the thoughts of our citizens towards a closer connection with her rival," Great Britain. All of these suggestions, particularly the last, had to "be managed with much delicacy" if the goal was to dissuade France from proceeding with its plan to recover Louisiana.[23]

If the retrocession had "irrevocably taken place," then a different course would have to be followed. Madison provided Livingston with clear instructions for just such a contingency. In that case, "sound policy" called for "nothing [to] be said or done which [would] unnecessarily irritate our future neighbours, or check the liberality which they may be disposed to exercise in relation to the trade and navigation through the mouth of the Mississippi." Instead, the government should "patronize the interests of our Western fellow citizens, by cherishing in France every just and liberal disposition towards their commerce." The United States would insist upon the rights secured to it by the Treaty of San Lorenzo—the use of the river to the Gulf of Mexico and the right of deposit in New Orleans. But France might also accept more advantageous arrangements than those already settled with Spain, such as the right to station a consul in New Orleans. Livingston should also try to induce France "to make over to the United States the Floridas … or at least West Florida." If France had not received the Floridas, Madison wanted Livingston to attempt to "dispose her to favor" Pinckney's negotiations to acquire them directly from Spain.[24]

When Pinckney and Livingston arrived at their European posts in the fall of 1801, they found it difficult to apply Madison's carefully crafted instructions. Even though the existence of a retrocession treaty was hardly a secret, neither the Spanish nor the French government would discuss it officially with the new American ministers. The French foreign minister, as Livingston later remarked, "absolutely den[ied] that any [treaty] had been formed on the subject." Within just weeks of their arrival in Europe, Livingston and Pinckney had grown frustrated by their inability to make any progress. Pinckney decided that, since the treaty had already been concluded, little could be done in Madrid. Livingston quickly determined that Louisiana was "a very favorite measure" with the French government and looked to Spain and Great Britain for possible "obstacles." What was even more disturbing was his conclusion that the French government had neither affection nor sympathy for the United States. Livingston insisted that, contrary to the beliefs of many Americans, *it [had] nothing that can be called republican in its form & still less in its administration.* It must have amazed Jefferson and Madison as well to read "that *the change in the politicks of the united States is* not what [the French government] would have wished." Their initial response to the retrocession rumors had been based upon the opposite assumption—that a republican government in France would naturally desire improved relations with the new Republican administration in the United States.[25]

Jefferson responded to these discouraging dispatches from France and Spain with one of the most famous letters to emerge from the retrocession crisis. On April 18, 1802, Jefferson wrote a private letter to Livingston in which he outlined a perspective on the current crisis that seemed very different from the initial view. France's acquisition of Louisiana and the Floridas, the president noted, "completely reverses all the political relations of the United States, and will form a new epoch in our political course." France had been viewed "as our *natural friend*"; but its possession of these provinces changed everything. "There is on the globe one single spot," Jefferson explained, "the possessor of which is our natural and habitual enemy[—]New Orleans, through which the produce of three-eighths of our territory must pass to market." By "placing herself in that door," France had assumed an "attitude of defiance" toward the United States. "Feeble" and "pacific,"

Spain could have held the mouth of the Mississippi "quietly for years." But France and the United States could not possibly remain friendly if "they [met] in so irritable a position." "The day that France takes possession of New Orleans" would fix not only American hostility toward France, but also American alliance with its rival. "From that moment," Jefferson famously concluded, "we must marry ourselves to the British fleet and nation." Jefferson assured Livingston that his intention was not to threaten France, because the United States did not "seek or desire" this "state of things." France could prevent the "inevitable" only by abandoning Louisiana. But it could delay it, at least, and "remove the causes of jarring and irritation" by "ceding to us the island of New Orleans and the Floridas."[26]

If this letter is the most famous document produced by the retrocession crisis, it is probably also the most misleading, at least when taken out of context. To draw the correct conclusions from it, we need to recognize two of its pertinent features. First, it was sent as a private letter from Jefferson to Livingston. We might reasonably assume that a private letter from the president to one of his diplomats abroad would provide the most accurate and revealing insights into the

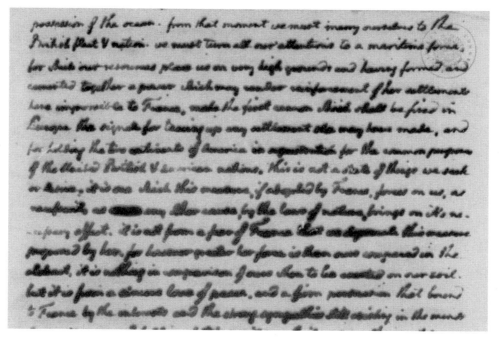

Detail from letter from Jefferson to Robert Livingston, April 18, 1802 (digitally enhanced). (Library of Congress)

administration's thinking. But that was not necessarily the case. A private letter, even from the president, was not viewed at the time as carrying the same weight as an official one. Jefferson's next letter to Livingston hinted as much: "I have got further into this matter than I meant when I began my letter of Apr. 18, not having deliberately intended to volunteer so far in the field of the Secretary of state." Second, this "private" letter to Livingston was intended for the eyes of the French government. Usually, such a momentous letter, whether private or official, would have been sent in code. But encoding it would have defeated Jefferson's plans. Even before writing the letter, he had arranged for Pierre Samuel DuPont de Nemours, a French immigrant who was going to Paris, to deliver it. The president intended for his wealthy friend to read the unsealed letter. In fact, he practically *instructed* DuPont to read it so that he could "impress on the government of France the inevitable consequences of their taking possession of Louisiana." Obviously, Jefferson could have simply written his "marry ourselves to the British fleet" letter to DuPont in the first place. But he must have calculated that such sentiments would have more weight with Napoleon if expressed in a letter to Livingston.[27]

Such an understanding of the context of this letter suggests that it was intended more to manipulate Napoleon than to instruct Livingston. That said, it still points to a shift in the administration's approach to the retrocession crisis. Even if Jefferson and Madison had no real intention of "marry[ing them]selves to the British fleet and nation" (and they clearly did not), just raising the possibility marked a step away from the original idea of impressing upon France the diplomatic distance between the United States and Great Britain. To some extent, the decision to introduce the subject of Anglo-American accord—a subject that Madison had warned needed to "be managed with much delicacy" the preceding September—had been made for them. In the weeks before Jefferson's April 18 letter, the State Department had received dispatches from Livingston showing that he had acted, on his own discretion, to employ King to enlist Great Britain. Livingston urged King to use British opposition to the transfer of Louisiana to thwart French plans. But he wanted King to do so discretely, in order to maintain the desired illusion of distance between the United States and Great Britain.

On first reading about Livingston's bold gambit, Jefferson and Madison thought that their minister had taken too great a risk. "A confidential *resort to [Great Britain],*" Madison warned Livingston in mid-March, "may be *abused for the purpose of sowing jealousies* in *France* and thereby *thwart our object.*" In such a dangerous game, he noted, "*too much circumspection cannot be employed.*" Jefferson's mid-April letter to Livingston seemed to indicate that the administration had decided to join its ministers in this game. But Jefferson and Madison actually did something quite different. Livingston and King tried to involve Great Britain without France learning of their efforts. In contrast, Jefferson and Madison invoked the specter of Great Britain to France without ever involving it. They clearly recognized that Livingston and King's efforts would become embarrassing if known; but they must also have understood that these efforts could be compromising if successful. The British, they assumed, would not resolve an American crisis without expecting something in return—something that they did not want to pay. Jefferson's nominally "private," but effectively open, letter to Livingston sought to achieve the benefits of British involvement without paying any of the costs.[28]

It could only achieve this goal, however, if DuPont actually disclosed its contents to Napoleon or someone else high in the French government. But there is no evidence that he did. In fact, DuPont took offense at Jefferson's barely concealed threat to his native country. He warned the president that Napoleon would "be much more irritated than impressed by" the position taken in the letter to Livingston. Napoleon's advisors would tell him that the American position—"prefer[ing] a treaty which [gave them] land rather than a treaty which would guarantee [their] rights"—showed an ambitious spirit. The letter would only convince Napoleon that the United States sought "the conquest of Mexico" and, thereby, redouble his commitment to holding onto Louisiana as a shield for his Spanish ally. So, instead of successfully enlisting DuPont to convey his message to Napoleon, Jefferson found himself laboring to dispel what he described as DuPont's "false impressions of the scope of the [April 18] letter." He delayed his return to Monticello in early May in order "to scribble a line to explain some ideas which seem[ed] not to have impressed [DuPont] exactly as they exist[ed] in [his] mind."[29]

Eighteen months into Jefferson's presidency, little progress had been made in resolving the retrocession crisis. Questions still remained about the details, and even the existence, of the treaty. Writing to Gallatin from Monticello in the late summer of 1802, Jefferson considered it "probable" that France would take possession of Louisiana, but noted that no "man in America [had] undoubted authority that it" would. Livingston's and Pinckney's dispatches from Europe revealed that the confusion over whether the treaty included the Floridas existed not just in Washington, but also in Paris and Madrid. The administration, moreover, had not entirely abandoned its initial policy. Madison still hoped to "[divert] the French Government from its unwise project" in October 1802, long after Pinckney's and Livingston's discouraging initial reports reached Washington. And the administration still viewed the acquisition of New Orleans and the Floridas "on convenient terms" as "the happiest of issues" that could emerge from this "most perplexing of occurrences."[30]

Nor had the administration's concerns changed. Jefferson, his advisors, and his diplomats still did not view the French return to Louisiana as any kind of military threat. In his April 18 letter to Livingston, Jefferson remarked that France's power, however greater than that of the United States when "compared in the abstract," was "nothing in comparison of ours, when to be exerted on our soil." Livingston agreed, assuring Madison that "the Colonies that France might attempt to establish on the west side of the Missisippi would be too feeble to injure us." Instead, the administration worried about the effects of a French "neighbourhood," particularly when "a possession of the mouth of the Mississippi [was] to be added to other causes of discord." During this period, the ultimate danger was often left unstated. Instead of discussing the potential outcome, Madison wrote vaguely to Livingston of "the worst events" and to King of "very serious events." It was rare that someone expressed what all American policymakers saw—that control over the Mississippi would give France the leverage to detach the trans-Appalachian West from the union. Or, as Pinckney put it, if westerners thought "that it was to France they were to look for the permission to navigate & deposit & not to their own Government[,] it would be a most unfortunate [idea] indeed & might ultimately produce a Separation."[31]

Nor did American thinking about Louisiana change between the summer of 1801 and the fall of 1802. Jefferson and his advisors preferred Spanish ownership of the vast province beyond the river to that of any other power, including the United States. In July 1801, Madison assured the French minister in Washington, Louis-André Pichon, that the idea of the United States "crossing the Mississippi" should be "regard[ed] … as a phantom." Ten months later, he informed Pinckney that the administration was prepared to consider a "guaranty of [Spain's] territory beyond the Mississippi" in exchange for all of its "Territory including New Orleans on this side." Jefferson and Madison attached so much importance to acquiring the territory east of the river, and securing its use for western farmers, that they were willing not only to foreswear Louisiana for themselves, but also to help Spain defend it against any other power. The Mississippi, in this case, would then form "a natural and quiet boundary with Spain." Louisiana, Jefferson assured DuPont in May 1802, was not sought by "a single reasonable and reflecting man in the US." He admitted "that the day may come, when it would be thought of," but insisted that it was "a very distant one." "At present we should consider an enlargement of our territory beyond the Missisipi to be almost as great a misfortune as a contraction of [our territory] on this side."[32]

By the fall of 1802, American policymakers and diplomats had already identified forces that, barring unforeseen developments, seemed likely to resolve the retrocession crisis. The dispute between France and Spain over whether the Treaty of San Ildefonso included the Floridas could be counted upon to delay the transfer of the province. Peace between France and Great Britain, though recently arranged by the Treaty of Amiens, always had to be considered precarious. Given British opposition to a French return to North America, increased Anglo-French hostility could work a transformation. It already seemed obvious, moreover, that France's efforts to crush the decade-old revolt of slaves and free people of color in its Caribbean colony of Saint Domingue (later Haiti) were *like to be protracted.* Since France could only spare enough troops, funds, and transport either to occupy Louisiana or to subjugate Saint Domingue, the continued success of the revolution in the latter insured delays in taking possession of the former. With such forces in play, Livingston concluded that *time and change may work in our favor.*" In September, he admitted that "were it not for the *uneasiness it excites at home [Louisiana] would give* me none for I am persuaded that the whole will end in a relinquishment of the country [to Spain] and transfer of the Capital [New Orleans] to the United States."[33]

Chapter Five

NEW ORLEANS AND THE WEST, FALL 1802

In many ways, New Orleans in the early 1800s could not have been more different from Washington. New Orleans was already an old city, having been the capital of first French and later Spanish Louisiana for eighty years. A city of nearly eight thousand in 1802, it was home to one of the most ethnically and racially diverse populations in North America. Its residents could easily have been subdivided into a dozen different parts—European and American immigrants of half-a-dozen nationalities, French and Spanish creoles, recent French immigrants from Saint Domingue, Native Americans of a number of different local tribes, African slaves of varied backgrounds, and the mixed-race *gens de colour* who enjoyed more freedoms there than almost anywhere else. This polyglot port city was already a place of polish and refinement. Its streets, though unpaved, were wide, regular, and laid out in a grid pattern. Most of its buildings were brick, often covered with white lime. According to one American who visited the city in 1801, the finest of them, at three stories, was "superb … and would not disgrace even Washington"—faint praise indeed. Even at the dawn of the nineteenth century, New Orleans already had a reputation as a city of parties, balls, promenades, and horse races. After one ball, an American visitor noted that "the room was elegant, the ladies very beautiful, the music good, and everything that could render the evening amusing and agreeable was well adapted."[34]

Geography alone guaranteed that New Orleans would "rank among the most important emporiums of the commercial world." Its location along the Mississippi about one hundred miles from the Gulf made it the nexus between the internal, riverine trade of a vast, fertile watershed and the external, oceanic trade of the Atlantic world. It was possible for oceangoing vessels to go further upriver, to

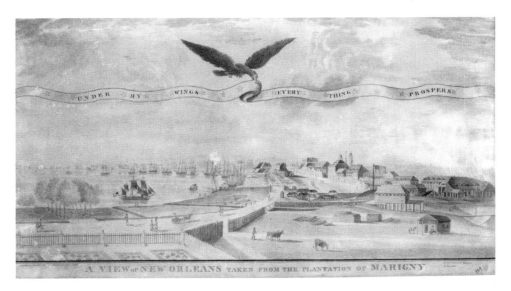

A View of New Orleans Taken from the Plantation of Marigny (1804) by John L. Boqueta de Woiseri. (Courtesy The Historic New Orleans Collection, Museum/ Research Center, Accession Number 1958.42)

Baton Rouge in Spanish West Florida or to Natchez in the Mississippi Territory. It was even possible to bypass all of the ports on the lower Mississippi; boatyards in Marietta and Pittsburgh began building ocean-going vessels—as much as two thousand miles from the Gulf—around 1801. But the majority of the downriver trade stopped at New Orleans's docks and was stored in its warehouses. Upriver transportation was so difficult before the age of steam that places like Pittsburgh, Marietta, Lexington, and Nashville received most of their supplies through the difficult, and expensive, overland route from Philadelphia. While ironwares, glass, china, books, and other relatively high-priced manufactured goods could be shipped overland at a profit, the West's low-price, high-bulk staples—corn, tobacco, wheat, pork, and hemp—could not. At least in 1802, western prosperity depended on the Mississippi route.[35]

Accordingly, westerners immediately took notice when Juan Ventura Morales, the Spanish intendant at New Orleans, suspended the American right of deposit in mid-October. Historians now know that Morales, the principal fiscal and commercial officer in the province, acted under secret orders from Madrid when he did so. What remains unclear is why these orders went out. Did the Spanish king and his advisors intend to help the French in some way or to harm them? At the time, no one in North America—not even the Spanish minister in Washington, Carlos Fernando Martínez de Yrujo, or Morales's immediate superior, the governor general of Louisiana—knew of these orders. Publicly and privately, Morales claimed that he had acted on his own authority to stop customs violations. He also asserted that he had not violated the Treaty of San Lorenzo because it had guaranteed the right of deposit only for three years—ignoring the fact that it also required Spain to provide alternate warehouse facilities if the deposit in New Orleans proved inconvenient. Recognizing the decree's significance, William E. Hūlings, the American vice consul in New Orleans, sent copies to the State Department using four different conveyances: two by sea through Baltimore, one by express, and a "quadruplicate by the Post via Natchez."[36]

The news of the intendant's decree produced first surprise and then outrage as it radiated out from New Orleans by land and sea. It reached Natchez in ten days, Frankfort, Kentucky, in a little under a month, and Chillicothe, Northwest Territory (where the Ohio statehood convention was meeting), just a few days later. A group of New Orleans merchants reported that this "Unexpected" and "extraordinary" event produced "the Utmost Confusion" in the city. The governor of the Mississippi Territory, William C. C. Claiborne, informed Madison that the news instantly "excited considerable agitation in Natchez and its vicinity." Within a week of learning of the decree, the Kentucky state legislature passed a memorial addressed to the president and Congress. That "Confusion" and "agitation" could quickly become something more forceful was clear from this memorial, which pledged to support "such measures as the honor, and interest of the United States [might] require" "at the expence of our lives and fortunes." Throughout the West, such war talk became common after the suspension of the deposit. The newly arrived customs collector in Natchez reported that New Orleans was "weak & this territory could alone take it in a week[,] which all Classes are anxious to try." According to a Virginian who had recently traveled beyond the mountains, westerners were "like a large combustible mass[—]they want only a Spark to set them on fire." "Either by treaty or by the sword," James Barbour warned the administration, they would secure themselves the use of the Mississippi.[37]

Most of these reports painted a picture of a bellicose West, one likely to engulf the nation in war with or without a formal declaration by Congress. "The People of that District," as one North Carolinian noted, were "a brave, hardy Race, not disposed to wait" and not easily restrained by the federal government. Even as they recognized the problems that western bellicosity and impetuosity might cause for the United States, most reporters on western conditions during this crisis insisted that westerners were firmly attached to the union, in general, and the Jefferson administration, in particular. But other views were sometimes expressed. Late in the crisis, Daniel Clark, the American consul in New Orleans, warned Jefferson and Madison that many westerners seemed "indifferent about their Country or at least indifferent about the effect French measures may produce on the Union." "No dependence ought to be placed on a majority of [westerners]," he insisted; they would "[secede] from the General Government" "if even very slight advantages were held out" by France.[38]

It was not only government officials—whether in Washington, in Europe, or in the West—who understood and articulated the danger of the retrocession as a threat to the union. William T. Barry, a nineteen-year-old law student in central Kentucky, shared Jefferson's and Madison's fears exactly. In a letter to his brother in May 1803, Barry argued that the possession of New Orleans by any power would be "prejudicial to our commercial interests." But, if it passed to "the French, an ambitious and enterprising people, it [would] involve the most serious consequences." Like Jefferson and Madison, Barry did not fear Napoleon's military might; he considered the idea that France would use Louisiana to "commence hostilities against Americans" to be "absurd." Instead, he worried that the French in Louisiana would "endeavour to extend their influence over the Western States and try to separate them from the Eastern." Their influence would derive from their control over "the sea ports on the Mississippi, which [were] the only marts for the commerce of [the West]." Once the French possessed New Orleans, they would "have hold of a lever with which they can wield and regulate our interests as they please," enabling them to foster "disunion between the Western and Eastern States."[39]

Chapter Six

'The Policy of Putting off the Day of Contention'

In his April 18, 1802, letter to Livingston, Jefferson had asserted that "every eye in the United States [was] now fixed on the affairs of Louisiana." "Nothing since the revolutionary war," he then suggested, "has produced more uneasy sensations through the body of the nation." When he wrote Livingston, Jefferson certainly overstated domestic sentiment, probably for the same reasons that he overstated his diplomatic calculations—to impress upon Napoleon the gravity of the situation. What was hyperbole in mid-April, though, was accurate by mid-December, when news of the suspension of the deposit had spread across the country. From the first rumors, the retrocession of Louisiana had produced occasional expressions of interest and concern in newspapers and private letters. Nonetheless, the administration had enjoyed considerable freedom to analyze the situation, decide its priorities, and implement its policies. All of this changed when the intendant effectively closed the Mississippi to most American trade. Now, the administration would need to respond to an intensified foreign crisis within a context of unprecedented domestic pressure from both the West and the opposition party.[40]

Jefferson and Madison developed their initial response to the new decree within days of receiving the first reports from New Orleans on November 25, three weeks before Congress convened. Immediately, they sent a formal protest to Yrujo, the Spanish minister, that urged him to use his influence to revoke the decree; Yrujo agreed to "[write] immediately on the subject to the local authority." Recognizing that Yrujo had no formal authority over the intendant, Madison also wrote to Pinckney during this initial flurry of activity, directing him to make "representations to the Spanish Government." Information from Hūlings and Yrujo convinced the administration that the intendant had acted on his own. Accordingly, Madison directed Pinckney to "presume" that Spain's distant agent had acted "contrary to its intentions." Even before this incident, Jefferson had complained about the "pigmy kings in [the European] colonies," who too often "[thought] proper to injure or insult us." But, despite their frustration at having "to dance across the ocean" for redress, Jefferson and Madison recognized that they needed to give Spain a chance to disavow the intendant's actions. With no reason "to impute this infraction to orders from the Spanish Government," the United States could not seek "redress, in the first instance, [in] the use of force."[41]

Jefferson did not simply await the result of this diplomacy. Beginning in December, he developed a new Indian policy that was shaped by the retrocession crisis. It was "becoming [an object] of great importance," in his view, to "[establish] a strong front on our Western boundary, the Missisipi." To achieve this goal, he considered it "all important to press on the Indians, as steadily and strenuously as they can bear, the extension of our purchases on the Mississippi." In the past, the government had tried to buy Indian land further east, closer to existing white settlements. But Jefferson wanted to prepare for a time when the United States might need either to defend itself against French Louisiana or, perhaps more likely, to seize New Orleans. By purchasing Indian lands on the eastern bank of the river and encouraging white settlement there, the government could "[plant] such a population on the Mississippi as [would] be able to do their own business, without the necessity of marching men from the shores of the Atlantic 1500 or 2000 miles thither, to perish by fatigue & change of climate." The means did not have to be pretty. Jefferson hoped to convince the Indians to abandon hunting in favor of "agriculture, … spinning and weaving," which required less land. But he was also willing to "push our trading houses" so that native leaders would run up large debts, since "when these debts get beyond what the individuals can pay, they become willing to lop them off by a cession of lands." And he urged the governors of the Indiana and Mississippi territories to act: "What ever can now be obtained must be obtained quickly." France's expected return to Louisiana was "already felt like a light breeze by the Indians" and would only "stiffen [them] against cessions of lands to us."[42]

When combined with the ongoing negotiations of Livingston and Pinckney, the diplomatic efforts to restore the deposit and the emerging plans for strengthening the western frontier seemed adequate for the present. Certainly, Jefferson did not invite any congressional involvement; his annual message opening the session entirely ignored the suspension of the deposit and barely mentioned Louisiana. When the House of Representatives requested information, Jefferson and Madison provided little and offered no encouragement for further congressional activity. In general, congressional Republicans seemed willing to follow this lead. But Federalists, in and out of Congress, condemned Jefferson's restraint. "In an emergency like the present," Hamilton insisted in late December, "Energy is Wisdom." But the administration could not act energetically, he believed, because of its "pretty scheme of substituting œconomy to taxation." At the same time, it could not preserve its "popularity ... with the Western partisans if their interests [were] tamely sacrificed." Hamilton captured the essence of Federalist thinking during the winter of 1802-1803: there were both national and party reasons to call for a military response. "The Unity of our empire and the best interests of our Nation," Hamilton argued, demanded seizing "all the territory East of the Mississippia." Federalist pressure for such an energetic response to the crisis, moreover, might pay political dividends in the overwhelmingly Republican West.[43]

The administration responded to domestic pressure, western and Federalist, by nominating Monroe as a special envoy to France and Spain in mid-January 1803. Jefferson clearly laid out the administration's thinking for his new minister. "The agitation of the public mind," he noted, "is extreme." In the West, such sentiments were "natural, and grounded on honest motives." But outside the West, in Jefferson's view, they were unnatural and dishonest. The "sea ports" wanted war only for the profits. The Federalists sought to force the administration into war "in order to derange our finances, or if this cannot be done, to attach the western country to them, as their best friends, and thus get again into power." The Monroe mission would answer the genuine concerns of westerners and, Jefferson hoped, thwart the devious efforts of the Federalists. All of the administration's previous measures had been "invisible," the president conceded. It was time for "something sensible"—something that could be seen and felt by westerners. Given the intended audience of the mission, Monroe was the best possible choice since he "possessed the unlimited confidence" of westerners due to his stand against the Jay-Gardoqui negotiations fifteen years earlier. By early February, Jefferson could already assert that, from the "moment" the mission was announced, "all [had] become quiet."[44]

But Jefferson's assertion, written when news of the mission was just beginning to reach the West, reflected nothing more than a hopeful prediction of the domestic response. With respect to western Republicans, it was largely correct. But the Federalists ridiculed the Monroe mission as "the weakest measure that ever disgraced the administration of any country." Hamilton was especially critical. In a New York newspaper, he assessed what he saw as the only available options: "to negotiate and endeavour to purchase, and if this fails to go to war," or "to seize at once on the Floridas and New-Orleans, and then negotiate." Certain that Napoleon would never sell, Hamilton advocated the latter option, an immediate military response. A week later, congressional Federalists attacked the administration's policies in the Senate. The lone western Federalist, Pittsburgh's James Ross, began with a fiery speech on February 14. Echoing Hamilton, he called for seizing New Orleans first, in order to "negotiate with more advantage." His speech introduced a series of resolutions that would have authorized the president to take possession of New Orleans and provided the militia and funds with which to do so. The Ross resolutions prompted three days of intense debate before finally being defeated by a slight majority. The Federalists must have known that they had little chance of passing and must have introduced them for other reasons. Embarrassing the administration was surely one. Accordingly, the Federalists insisted that the debates be opened to the public—and the press—despite the sensitivity of the issue. By granting the president discretionary authority rather than simply declaring war, moreover, the resolutions would have placed the responsibility for not using force on Jefferson.[45]

The Monroe mission was not merely a response to domestic pressure, however. It was also the administration's reaction to a new assessment of French plans for Louisiana. Long before the intendant issued his decree, Livingston and Pinckney had asked their respective hosts whether the Treaty of San Ildefonso had recognized the American rights fixed by the Treaty of San Lorenzo—to use the river and to deposit goods at New Orleans. Both had received reassuring verbal answers. But, despite repeated requests, neither the French nor Spanish governments had actually committed themselves in writing on this crucial point. After months of French avoidance, Livingston reported, in a letter that reached Washington on January 3, that the French viewed *the treaty as wastepaper.* He predicted an *early attempt to corrupt our western people.* Suspending the deposit had appeared to be the act of the intendant. But what if it was not? What if it was, instead, a glimpse of what was to come? To westerners, the Mississippi was "every thing," as Madison reminded Pinckney: "It is the Hudson, the Delaware, the Potomac and all the navigable rivers of the atlantic States formed into one stream." Their "interest" would always connect them to the power that controlled the river. This fact seemed to account for the French desire to recover Louisiana. Writing to Livingston and Monroe, Madison explained that France believed "that by holding the key to the commerce of the Mississipi, she [would] be able to command the interests and attachments of the Western portion of the United States." In that position, France could "either controul the Atlantic portion also" or "seduce the [West] into a separate Government, and a close alliance with herself."[46]

Jefferson and Madison clearly fixed the diplomatic goal of the Monroe mission. "The object," Madison wrote, was "to procure a cession of New Orleans and the Floridas to the United States and consequently the establishment of the Mississippi as the boundary between the United States and Louisiana." Over and over, in official documents and private letters, Jefferson and Madison reiterated this goal. They were not looking beyond the river, which was perfectly satisfactory as a western boundary. Owning the eastern bank of the Mississippi to the Gulf, including the existing port at New Orleans, would meet western demands. Acquiring the Floridas, moreover, would protect the interests of future settlers on the other rivers that flowed into the Gulf from Georgia and the Mississippi Territory. Information from Livingston and DuPont encouraged Jefferson and Madison to believe that a purchase was possible. It was only necessary to decide *the sum of money to be thrown* into the transaction." DuPont had suggested six million dollars. But the administration *hoped that less [would] do.*" In the end, the instructions for Livingston and Monroe accepted DuPont's figure. But they also divided the purchase into its components in case only a partial deal was possible: four-and-a-half million dollars for the island of New Orleans, one million for West Florida, and half-a-million for East Florida. Given their concerns, it made perfect sense that the tiny island of New Orleans, just a few hundred square miles, would be worth nine times as much as the entirety of modern Florida.[47]

The instructions for Livingston and Monroe demonstrated that the administration could imagine a number of resolutions to the crisis that were preferable to immediate war. Purchasing all of the French and Spanish claims east of the Mississippi was the optimal solution. But Jefferson and Madison also thought that the crisis could be alleviated by purchasing just New Orleans or just the two Floridas or just West Florida. They would even settle for "as large a portion" of the island of New Orleans as France would agree to sell. "Should no considerable portion of it be attainable," Madison continued, "it will still be of vast importance to get a jurisdiction over space enough for a large commercial town and its appurtenances, on the banks of the river" near its mouth. Thus, if France would not sell the city of New Orleans, the United States would build its own port, from scratch, at the lower end of the river. If France would not sell any territory along the Mississippi, the instructions called for the ministers to clarify "the present right of deposit" and expand it by adding the privileges of owning real estate in New Orleans and of "having Consuls residing there." Madison warned that "the United States [could] not remain satisfied, nor the Western people be kept patient," with any less.[48]

As low as the administration had set its minimum demands, Madison's warning reads as ridiculous bluster at first glance. But we should read it, instead, as a clue to the administration's thinking—one that can be combined with other evidence from private letters. This evidence shows that Jefferson and Madison identified two crucial dividing points in their array of proposals and options. The first separated peace from war; the second divided *eventual* from *immediate* war. If the two ministers could acquire at least New Orleans or West Florida, then the United States would "insure to ourselves a course of perpetual peace and friendship with all nations." If they failed to do so, yet managed to make any of the other arrangements authorized by their instructions, they would at least buy time for further preparations and negotiations before eventual military action became necessary. If Livingston and Monroe could not secure Madison's minimum demands, however, then the administration would need to plan for *immediate* war. Accepting even the possibility of the closure of the river or the suspension of the deposit was unthinkable. "The use of the Mississippi [is] so indispensable," Jefferson informed DuPont, "that we cannot hesitate one moment to hazard our existence for its maintenance."[49]

In the early spring of 1803, Jefferson and Madison saw ample grounds for patience and restraint. All of the news from Europe made a renewed Anglo-French war seem imminent. Such a war would make France both more likely to sell and less able to defend New Orleans; it would also allow the United States to secure British cooperation on easier terms. Furthermore, French efforts to regain control over Saint Domingue were in a "disastrous state," as Madison noted. Yellow fever had decimated the French troops on the island, taking the commanding general along with countless others. Unless France intended "to abandon the reduction of that Island," it would not have enough troops to take possession of Louisiana. Domestic considerations suggested the value of patience as well, at least to the administration. Time would allow for reducing the national debt, encouraging settlement along the Mississippi, and, generally, "obtain[ing] more of that strength which is growing on us so rapidly." Reports from New Orleans that the intendant, on orders from Madrid, had revoked his decree seemed to confirm the wisdom of negotiation. In the president's view, peaceful means had quickly accomplished what the favorite policy of "our federal maniacs" could have won only with "7. years of war, 100,000 human lives, 100 millions of additional debt, besides ten hundred millions lost by the want of market for our produce, and the general demoralizing of our citizens which war occasions." Admitting that he was not confident of "obtaining New Orleans from France for money," Jefferson insisted that he remained "confident in the policy of putting off the day of contention."[50]

Despite the transformative effects of the suspension of the deposit, despite the new pressures from the West and in Congress, despite the new concerns about French intentions, Jefferson and Madison remained consistent in their thinking about that part of Louisiana—the vast majority—west of the Mississippi. Over and over, in their instructions to Livingston and Monroe, in their letters to friends and supporters, and in their conversations with foreign diplomats, they referred to the Mississippi as the desired western boundary of the United States. What they were saying, of course, was that they hoped to acquire everything east of the river. But what they were not saying was that they wanted to acquire anything west of the river. The administration knew very little about Louisiana west of the river; finding out more formed a leading motive for the Lewis and Clark Expedition, which was proposed in January 1803 and was being planned and prepared throughout the spring. Louisiana's vast—and, to their minds, empty—spaces had begun to seem like a vacuum, one that was likely to be filled by something threatening. They would have been thrilled to see it back in Spanish hands since, as King put it, "they were quiet neighbours." Instead, the French were readying themselves to take possession. A French Louisiana could be reconciled with American interests, if New Orleans and the Floridas were sold or ceded to the United States. But the French seemed certain to draw in the British. Even if the British just claimed Upper Louisiana, north of the Missouri River, *the evils involved in such an extension of her possessions in our neighborhood and in such a hold on the Mississippi [were] obvious.* The prospect of the British filling the vacuum of Louisiana, Madison insisted, was *altogether repugnant to the sentiments and sound policy of the United States.*[51]

The thought of a British Louisiana, unlike that of a French Louisiana, led at least one cabinet member to consider American expansion beyond the Mississippi. After reviewing Jefferson's draft instructions for the Lewis and Clark Expedition, Gallatin suggested revealing additions. Jefferson saw the expedition largely in commercial and scientific terms—as a search for "the most direct & practicable water communication across this continent for the purposes of commerce" and a survey of the cultures, animals, plants, minerals, and climate along this route. To Gallatin, "the present aspect of affairs" in the spring of 1803 suggested additional goals. Calculating that it might "ere long" be "necessary" for the United States to "[take] immediate possession, [to] prevent G[reat] B[ritain] from doing the same," he viewed the expedition as an opportunity for a military reconnaissance of Upper Louisiana. But Gallatin also looked beyond "the present difficulties." The

Missouri Valley, he believed, was "perhaps the only large tract of country, and certainly the *first*," outside of the existing union that would "be settled by the people of the United States." As such, he wanted to learn about the fertility of the soil, the "evenness" of the land, and the natural boundaries of the watershed. "The great object," in his view, was to determine "whether from its extent and fertility that country [was] susceptible of a large population in the same manner as the corresponding tract on the Ohio." Was Gallatin confident or concerned—confident that the United States would acquire the Missouri country, which it would be happy to learn was fertile and extensive, or concerned that a fertile and extensive Missouri country, even if filled by "the people of the United States," would form a dangerous neighbor outside the union? When he reminded Jefferson that "the future destinies of the Missouri country [were] of vast importance to the United States," was he expressing hope or fear?[52]

Vue de la Nouvelle Eglise de Ste. Geneviève, de Paris, *engraved by Roger after Testard. (Thomas Jefferson Foundation, Inc.)*

Chapter Seven

PARIS, SPRING 1803

In 1803, Paris was just beginning an era of sweeping change. In many ways, it remained a medieval city at the dawn of the nineteenth century. Most of its population of half-a-million people lived in old buildings on narrow, twisting streets. Over the previous fifteen years, Paris had experienced all of the promise, all of the turmoil, and all of the violence of the French Revolution. Churches and universities had been destroyed; palaces had been thrown open to the people. But the Revolution had not managed to reshape the city into something modern. Napoleon, who was the first consul—not yet the emperor—in the spring of 1803, envisioned something much grander. He expected Paris to be the center of a vast empire. Accordingly, Napoleon called for new palaces, museums, monuments, and public spaces to serve as symbols of France's new glory. He also placed the resources of the nation behind improving the infrastructure of the city—newly paved streets, new water and sewage systems, new quays on the Seine, new granaries, and new factories. In the spring of 1803, only the first steps had been taken, but an era of expectancy and excitement had begun.

What most impressed Livingston, who had been in Paris since December 1801, was the splendor and ceremony of Napoleon's court. In his first dispatch to Washington, Livingston had described at length the formality, grandeur, and militarism of *"the present ceremonial."* His account of the monthly parade of "5000 of the finest troops in the world" and monthly audience for all of the foreign ministers and ambassadors with the first consul was meant to suggest how far Napoleonic France had strayed from republican principles. By the fall of 1802, Livingston had entirely abandoned the idea that France was a republic. "There never was a government," he warned Madison, "in which *less* could be done *by negotiation than here*. There is *no people no legislature no counselors[.] One man* is every thing." Livingston considered Napoleon's ministers *"mere clerks"* and his counselors *"parade officers."*[53]

Photogravure of Charles-Maurice de Talleyrand by Goupil and Co. (Courtesy Louisiana State Museum, gift of Gilbert Fortier III)

Accordingly, Livingston directed his efforts toward bringing his government's concerns and proposals directly under the eye of the first consul. Protocol dictated that Livingston work through the foreign minister, Charles-Maurice de Talleyrand-Périgord, but Talleyrand seemed too reluctant to challenge Napoleon's imperial vision for Louisiana. So Livingston abandoned the formal channel through the foreign minister in favor of the informal ones that always existed around courts. Dinners and balls exposed him to the men who might be able to influence Napoleon, particularly the first consul's brother, Joseph. Livingston never stopped sending formal letters to Talleyrand, but he decided that more could be accomplished with informal notes to Joseph Bonaparte. Progress toward resolving the crisis over Louisiana seemed more likely at "a Shooting party at [Joseph's] country house" than an official meeting at Talleyrand's office.[54]

It could hardly have come as a surprise then, when, on the evening of April 12, 1803, Livingston looked up from the dinner table and saw "the Minister of the Treasury walking in [his] garden." François Barbé-Marbois had gone to Livingston's house to elicit an American proposal to purchase New Orleans and all of Louisiana. Livingston had just sat down to dine with Monroe—who had finally arrived in Paris that day—and "Several other Gentlemen." Barbé-Marbois returned after dinner, joined the company for coffee, and, after "Stroll[ing] into the next room" with Livingston, invited the minister to "call upon him" later that evening. Once Monroe and the other guests "took leave," Livingston followed Barbé-Marbois to the treasury office. That a resolution to the crisis would come through the finance minister, rather than the foreign minister, and that it would be initiated in a private home, rather than a government office, would hardly have surprised Livingston after eighteen months at Napoleon's court. That the "First Consul was disposed to Sell" the entirety of Louisiana, however, was certainly a shock. The previous day, Talleyrand had asked Livingston whether the United States wanted the entire province, pressing the American to know what his government "'would give for the whole.'" But Livingston did not treat the offer as a serious one, in part because of his doubts that Talleyrand had any influence with Napoleon. When Barbé-Marbois raised the issue again the next evening, Livingston "plainly Saw the whole business"— Napoleon really did want to sell all of Louisiana.[55]

François Barbé-Marbois by Isnard Osicran. (Courtesy Louisiana State Museum)

Why did Napoleon suddenly decide to sell the entirety of Louisiana to the United States? Historians have pointed to a number of factors, all of which were probably involved to some degree. Clearly, the growing likelihood of a new war with Great Britain was one of the most important. Napoleon recognized that, once the war began, it would be impossible for France to occupy Louisiana and then defend it from Great Britain. If the British seized it, they could be expected to use it as a base to attack the Spanish colonies throughout the New World. Selling Louisiana to the United States would keep the province out of British hands and bring in much-needed gold on the eve of the war. Mollifying the Americans on this explosive issue would also help to insure that they remained neutral in the war. The continuing setbacks in Saint Domingue probably contributed to the decision to abandon Louisiana as well. Napoleon had viewed Louisiana as one part of a French economic system in the Western Hemisphere. It would produce the wheat, corn, rice, beef, lumber, and barrel staves that would allow the planters of the French West Indies to devote all of their land, and their slaves' labor, to the vastly more profitable sugar. If France could not regain control and restore slavery in Saint Domingue, then Louisiana's staples would be less valuable. Another factor that may have influenced Napoleon's decision was the various signs of deepening American concern about the future of New Orleans, including the Monroe mission, the Ross resolutions in Congress, and the public meetings in the West.

Within hours of visiting Barbé-Marbois's office, Livingston had decided that the United States should buy Louisiana. He had not conferred with Monroe, and apparently had not even read the instructions that Monroe had brought from Washington, when he made this decision. But, by 3:00 a.m. on April 13, he felt confident enough in his decision to inform the secretary of state: "We Shall do all we can to *cheapen the purchase but my present sentiment is that we shall buy.*" Over the next two weeks, Livingston, Monroe, and Barbé-Marbois tried to come to an agreement on price and other terms. Barbé-Marbois had initially stated that Napoleon wanted one hundred million livres (close to nineteen million dollars), with the United States assuming the claims of American merchants against the French government. When Livingston balked at "the extreme exorbitancy of the demand," the finance minister quickly countered with sixty million livres plus another twenty million to cover the claims. Livingston and Monroe's intention to "cheapen the purchase" soon collided with their recognition that the transaction would become infinitely more complicated if the negotiations were still ongoing when the expected Anglo-French war began. On April 30, they agreed to a draft treaty that fixed the price for Louisiana at sixty million livres ($11,250,000), with another twenty million ($3,750,000) in assumed damage claims. Livingston and Monroe agreed to spend two-and-a-half times what they had been authorized to spend to buy a province that they had never been instructed to buy.[56]

In their haste to sign, Livingston and Monroe accepted a treaty that deviated in many particulars from their instructions. Gallatin had detailed all of the financial terms regarding both the purchase and the assumed claims; Livingston and Monroe ignored Gallatin's payment plan and accepted a claims convention that was so sloppy that it caused problems for decades. Madison had been willing to grant France ten years of preferential trading terms; the treaty extended this period to twelve years. Madison had very carefully defined the boundaries of the various places that he wanted to purchase; the actual treaty specified neither the eastern nor the western boundary of Louisiana. And, in his outline for the treaty,

Madison had explained that the administration could not commit the government to extend full citizenship or promise statehood to the inhabitants of the purchased territory, though he suggested that "it [was] to be expected from the character and policy of the United States that such incorporation [would] take place without unnecessary delay." Livingston and Monroe accepted a clause that obligated the United States to incorporate the people of Louisiana on equal terms as soon as possible under the Constitution. In time, all of the deviations that Livingston and Monroe accepted in Paris created difficulties for the United States.[57]

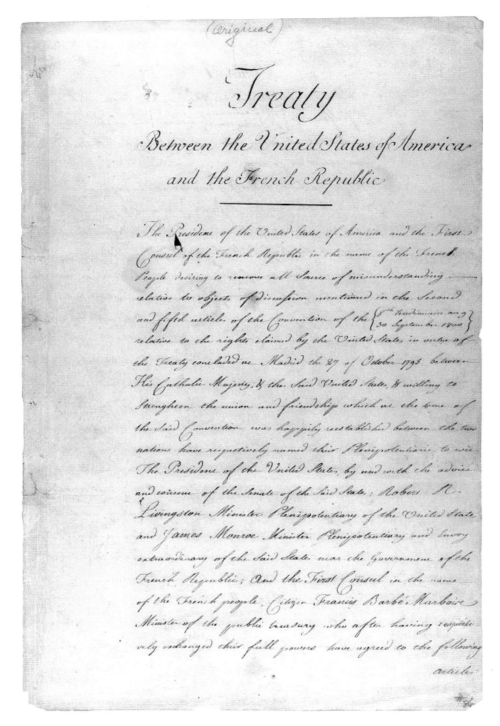

Page one of the English language version of the Louisiana Purchase Treaty, April 30, 1803. (National Archives)

Chapter Eight

'IT MAY EVEN BE A SUBJECT OF DISQUIETUDE'

Livingston and Monroe clearly understood that the result and the process of their negotiations were likely to be controversial at home. It was not at all certain that the administration would approve of their decision to acquire, and to spend, so much more than it had authorized. Accordingly, they filled their official dispatches to the State Department and their private letters to Madison and others with extended justifications of their actions. Even if Jefferson and Madison approved of the treaty, the public might not. In a letter to King, Livingston acknowledged his doubts about "the opinion of the present day," while insisting that he would "stake [his] political character with posterity upon this treaty." Finally, even if the people in general approved of the purchase, the Federalists seemed almost certain to oppose it. "I shall not be surprised," Monroe wrote Madison in a private letter, "to hear that many of those who were ready to plunge into war for a light portion of what is obtained, shod. now take another course and declaim agnst the govt. & its agents for getting too much." The Federalists, he warned, would "imagine" "evils … [in] the immensity of the acquisition."[58]

What is most striking about the responses to the Louisiana Purchase— whether on the part of Livingston and Monroe, or the administration, or western Republicans, or eastern Federalists—is how frequently they derived from the same understanding of the problem of neighborhood and the solution of union that had shaped American thinking about the West for two decades. Supporters of the purchase expected countless benefits from it, but removing a potentially dangerous neighbor and strengthening an admittedly tenuous union were regularly included among them. Opponents of the purchase discovered numerous defects in the treaty. But they almost always warned that the purchase would destroy the union and create a powerful and dangerous neighbor in the West. Today, the Federalists' fears may seem incomprehensible. But Jefferson, Madison, Monroe, and many others who approved of the Louisiana Purchase understood and, to some extent, shared them. If they ultimately downplayed these fears, they never simply dismissed them. Instead, they sought policies to prevent the threatening developments that the opponents of the purchase predicted.

Livingston and Monroe tried to shape the domestic response to their actions, the administration's policies, and the purchase itself with their official letter announcing and accompanying the treaty—a letter that they could have reasonably expected would have been published along with the treaty. In it, they explained both the "Circumstances" that had made obeying their instructions impossible and the "Considerations" that had induced them to buy all of Louisiana. "Mr. Marbois was absolutely restricted to the disposition of the whole," they assured Madison; it was "useless" to press for less. Even as they admitted that they had purchased far more than the administration had authorized, they argued that their treaty squared with "the wise and benevolent Policy of our Government." Purchasing all of Louisiana would go even further than purchasing New Orleans and the Floridas to secure American trade down the Mississippi. It would also address the problem of "neighbourhood" by eliminating the danger of future collisions with whatever power owned the western bank of the river. As the suspension of the deposit had shown, "a capricious, unfriendly or unprincipled subaltern" in such a colony could easily "wound our best interests, violate our most unquestionable Rights, and involve us in war." "By this acquisition," Livingston and Monroe argued, such dangers were "banished for ages from the U. states." The purchase, they predicted, would distance the United States "from the European World & its concerns, especially its wars & intrigues," and strengthen "the Bond of our Union."[59]

But the domestic response to the Louisiana Purchase began long before the publication of Livingston and Monroe's carefully crafted justification; in fact, it began before the arrival of the treaty itself. On July 5, Hamilton fired one of the first of many Federalist salvos against the negotiations and the purchase in an unsigned essay in the *New-York Evening Post*. Though happy that the crisis had "terminated favourably to this country," he criticized both the means and the result. The purchase, Hamilton argued, had resulted "solely [from] a fortuitous concurrence of unforseen and unexpected circumstances, and not [from] any wise or vigorous measures on the part of the American government." He still thought that Jefferson should have acted energetically when the Spanish intendant suspended the right of deposit. Instead, the administration had negotiated. As Hamilton saw it, without the "obstinate resistance" of the "black inhabitants" of Saint Domingue and the clear warnings of the British, France would have occupied Louisiana and the United States would have tasted "the fruits of our folly." "Absolutely compelled by [his] situation," Napoleon had decided to sell.[60]

But what had the United States acquired? Hamilton was sure that the treaty included nothing east of the Mississippi except the island of New Orleans. Like the administration in the months before the purchase, he thought that the crisis could have been resolved without looking beyond the river: "The acquisition of New-Orleans [would have been] perfectly adequate to every purpose." The best that could be said of "the immense, undefined region west of the river," in Hamilton's view, was that Spain wanted it and might be induced to "barter" it "for the Floridas." It certainly was not needed for "actual settlement" and would not be "for many years, if not centuries to come." But the great danger, according to Hamilton, was that this "wilderness" would not remain unsettled. "Our own citizens," whom he described as "more enterprizing than wise," would soon emigrate to Louisiana. Hamilton predicted two equally alarming outcomes: "the dismemberment of a large portion of our country, or a dissolution of the Government." Either all of the West beyond the Appalachians would leave the union, or the addition of new states beyond the Mississippi would destroy the original sectional balance of the Constitution. "On the whole," Hamilton concluded, it was "extremely problematical" "whether the possession at this time of any territory west of the river Mississippi [would] be advantageous."[61]

In letters, essays, and speeches, other Federalists echoed and extended Hamilton's analysis. Even those who approved the result of the treaty denied the administration, and often even the negotiators, any credit for it. They argued that their own approach would have acquired all that the nation needed at less expense.

They denounced the treaty as unconstitutional because it committed the United States to incorporate Louisiana on equal terms. And they warned that such incorporation would destroy the sectional balance of the union by "throw[ing] N. England quite into the background." But they also returned over and over to the idea that the purchase would lead necessarily to the fragmentation of the union. "The possession of that immense territory," New Hampshire Senator William Plumer concluded, "will hasten the dissolution of our present government. We must form different empires." Some Federalists, including Plumer, expected the purchase to "precipitate" New Englanders into "erect[ing] a seperate & independent Empire." Others warned that it would bring about the very division at the Appalachians that Jefferson and Madison had labored to prevent. Americans would soon find that, "instead of having advanced to *Mexico,* [they had] *lost all beyond the Alleghany.*" Or, they projected that American settlement beyond the Mississippi, which could be prevented only by "a cordon of troops," would end in a separate, American empire beyond the Mississippi. As one writer explained, the truly dangerous neighbors were not "European settlements[,] but ... such as our own indiscretion may plant and cherish." Through whatever means, the Louisiana Purchase seemed certain to *"[lay] an everlasting foundation for exhausting blood and treasure in America, as they are wasted in Europe—by neighboring nations for the destruction of each other."* [62]

Though not surprised by Federalist criticism, Jefferson took a very different view of the purchase. The precise terms of the treaty might not have been what the administration intended. But it was no accident, in his view, that the negotiations ended in the acquisition of territory that secured American rights on the Mississippi. Federalist "grumblers" would be "cruelly mortified," he wrote one supporter, if they could see the administration's "files from May, 1801," and "more especially from April, 1802." They would learn that, "though we could not say when war would arise [in Europe], yet we said with energy what would take place when it [did]." Jefferson knew that the files of the State and War Departments would show that, even as the cabinet hoped that negotiations in Paris and Madrid would suffice, it had quietly prepared for war, by promoting settlement along the eastern bank of the Mississippi and considering cooperation with Great Britain. The Federalist alternative of immediate war, the president believed, would only have brought on the "catastrophe" that the administration was working so hard to avoid.[63]

For Jefferson, the result of the administration's policies proved the wisdom of its approach. Like the Federalists, he did not think that Louisiana would need to be opened for settlement for generations; it did promise "to our posterity," however, "a noble prospect of provision for ages." But Jefferson never doubted, as many Federalists did, that obtaining all of Louisiana was better than just acquiring the island of New Orleans. The latter "would of itself have been a great thing," he informed one supporter, since it would have secured trade on the Mississippi. But the acquisition of Louisiana was "inappreciable." No longer would the United States share the river with a potentially hostile neighbor. As such, the purchase would prevent "those bickerings with foreign powers" that seemed certain to lead to war. This analysis led Jefferson to reject without hesitation Hamilton's, and other Federalists', argument that Louisiana west of the river should be exchanged with Spain for the Floridas. Confident that the United States would acquire the Floridas in any case, he insisted that such an exchange would needlessly "let Spain into the Mississippi," breeding future quarrels over its use. Like Livingston and Monroe, Jefferson found in the Louisiana Purchase a promise of permanent peace for the United States; it would "[secure] to us the course of a peaceable nation."[64]

Others in the administration shared the president's general perspective. Like Jefferson, they championed the purchase for securing western trade and preventing future conflicts. Gallatin even argued that Jefferson's enumeration of the benefits of the purchase, particularly in his October 1803 message to Congress, failed to make clear one of the most critical. The acquisition, Gallatin noted, was "a most solid bond of the Union." To Madison, "the uses to which [Louisiana might] be turned, render[ed] it a truly noble acquisition." Properly managed, it could "do much good as well as … prevent much evil." By removing France from the nation's frontiers, it would allow for a smaller "military establishment"—"saving expence & favoring liberty." Taking a broader view, Madison suggested that the purchase could permanently remove the danger of a hostile neighbor beyond the Mississippi. It took "the regulation & settlement of that territory out of other hands," whether French, Spanish, or British, and put them "into those of the U.S."

Like Jefferson, Monroe, and many others, Madison did not think that the government should immediately allow Americans to settle the region. But he was heartened that the United States, not some other power, would "manage both [regulation and settlement] for the general interest & conveniency."[65]

Western Republicans displayed their pleasure with Livingston and Monroe's handiwork in public meetings, newspaper essays, and private letters. More than most Americans, they celebrated the Louisiana Purchase as a multifaceted and unalloyed boon to the nation, as a whole, and their region, in particular. Few evinced any doubts about either the process or the result. Cincinnati's John Smith, who had been chosen as one of Ohio's first senators, echoed administration thinking by arguing that it was "much better [to] pay a large sum in a fair purchase, then in a long & bloody war." According to the optimistic appraisal of western Republicans, the acquisition of Louisiana would secure trade, preserve peace, and destroy faction. Governor Claiborne argued that "the tranquility and security of all the Western Country [were] now secured to an incalculable distance of time." Westerners did not necessarily view Louisiana as a new field for immediate settlement. "The advantage of this Cession to our generation," Smith noted in language similar to Jefferson's, "will be small and inconsiderable, compared with what it will be in future." At present, it mattered most as a cement of union and a buffer against neighbors. Westerners would see their interests and rights promoted and protected "under the patronage of the general Government," "conciliat[ing] their affections ... and confirm[ing] their hopes and confidence" in union with the East. And, possessing "both sides" of the Mississippi, the United States, as one westerner confidently asserted, ran "no risk from bad Neighbors."[66]

In some ways, the differences between Federalist opponents and Republican supporters of the Louisiana Purchase were not as sharp as they appear. Jefferson, his advisors in Washington, and his negotiators in Paris operated within the same understanding of union and neighborhood that made the purchase so worrisome to so many Federalists. In a private letter to Monroe, Madison admitted that, "in some views," the purchase might "even be a subject of disquietude." Like many Federalists, Jefferson and his supporters recognized the allure of new lands beyond the Mississippi for would-be farmers throughout the United States. Like many

Federalists, they worried that settlers beyond the river would prove ungovernable, making them likely to set up new governments of their own outside of the union. And, like many Federalists, they feared that an independent nation in the western half of the Mississippi watershed would draw to it the American states and territories in the eastern half, including Kentucky, Tennessee, and Ohio. But Jefferson and his supporters believed that they could guard against the inherent dangers with measures less radical than the one most commonly proposed by the Federalists—returning all of Louisiana, except New Orleans, to Spain in exchange for the Floridas. In their earliest reactions to the purchase, Jefferson, Madison, Monroe, and others in the administration all wrote of Louisiana as a problem that could, and needed to, be managed. In their minds, "plac[ing] the new accession of Louisiana on proper grounds"—as Jefferson put it—required preventing its settlement far into the future.[67]

But would the vast expanses of Louisiana ultimately become a part of the American union? Federalist concerns forced Jefferson to address this critical question, first in private letters and later in public messages. Surprisingly, his responses—to Kentucky Senator John Breckinridge in August 1803, to English radical Joseph Priestley in January 1804, and finally to Congress and the public in March 1805—clashed with the logic that had shaped both American politics for two decades and his own policies toward the retrocession. He claimed to view with equanimity the idea of an independent nation, settled by Americans, either beyond the Mississippi or beyond the Appalachians. "The future inhabitants of the Atlantic and Mississippi States will be our sons," he informed Breckinridge; "if they see their interest in separation, why should we take side with our Atlantic rather than our Mississippi descendants?" To Priestley, Jefferson made an amazing assertion: it was "not very important to the happiness of either part ... whether we remain in one confederacy, or form into Atlantic and Mississippi confederacies."[68]

Had Jefferson's thinking really changed so suddenly and so completely? The simple answer is "not really." For one thing, his comments need to be understood in the context of Federalist proposals for exchanging Louisiana for the Floridas. He reversed the Federalists' nightmarish portrayal of the future, in part, to remove the foundation for their policies. Jefferson looked to a much later period—"in future time," as he wrote Priestley—than the Federalists did for his optimistic vision of a separation. By then, ties of kinship, language, trade, and principles would make it "likely," though not certain, that the resulting nations could "live in harmony and friendly intercourse." Finally, Jefferson's expressions of equanimity about a separation often accompanied statements that were more consistent with his earlier ideas and policies. "We have seldom seen neighborhood produce affection among nations," he reminded Breckinridge in the midst of his discussion of a future separation. "The reverse is almost the universal truth."[69]

Chapter Nine

WASHINGTON AND MONTICELLO, SUMMER 1803

For Jefferson and his cabinet, perhaps the first question to consider once the news of the treaty reached Washington in early July 1803 was: "Is it constitutional?" Throughout the 1790s, the Republicans had criticized the Federalists for the freedom with which they interpreted the Constitution. Jefferson, Madison, and Gallatin had condemned Hamilton, Washington, and Adams for using the "general welfare" and "necessary and proper" clauses as the constitutional basis for a national bank and other measures. To Republicans, the language of the Constitution had to be strictly construed, and the Tenth Amendment—which reserved to the states and the people all of the powers that were not explicitly granted to the federal government by the Constitution—had to be taken seriously. Could Republican "strict constructionism" accommodate the purchase of Louisiana and the pledge to incorporate its people within the union? During the summer of 1803, this question sparked a serious debate within the government over the need for a constitutional amendment.

The debate had actually begun in January, as the plans for the Monroe mission took shape. At that time, the purchase was expected to include, at most, New Orleans and the Floridas. Even so, Attorney General Levi Lincoln saw great constitutional problems in any agreement with France or Spain that promised to add these provinces to the American union as equal states. He accepted the general wisdom that the union, "when formed, was predicated on the then existing *united* States, and such as could grow out of *them*, & out of *them* only." Trying "to amend the constitution, [so] as to embrace the object," seemed risky given the confirmed hostility of the Federalists. To circumvent this problem, Lincoln proposed annexing the purchased provinces to existing states and territories—East Florida to

Georgia and West Florida and New Orleans to the Mississippi Territory. Simply purchasing the territory and admitting it into the union, Lincoln warned, might be viewed as a dangerous "precedent." A "future executive" might extend this precedent "to the purchase of Louisiana, or still further south, & become the Executive of the United States of North & South America." In a letter to Jefferson, Gallatin flatly rejected Lincoln's position, arguing that "the existence of the United States as a nation presuppose[d] the power enjoyed by every nation of extending their territory by treaties." Gallatin also thought that the Constitution already permitted the admission of new territories into the union, though he was not "perfectly satisfied" on this point. After weighing both sides, Jefferson decided that there was "no constitutional difficulty as to the acquisition of territory." Whether the purchase could be incorporated into the union without an amendment would be "a question of expediency." Still, as he saw matters in mid-January, it seemed "safer" to require one.[70]

Accordingly, as soon as the news of the Louisiana Purchase reached Washington in July, Jefferson drafted a constitutional amendment and circulated it among those cabinet members who were in the capital—Madison, Gallatin, and

Front View of the President's House in the City of Washington, *1807, by Charles William Janson. Detail from the title page of* The Stranger in America. *(Courtesy White House Historical Association)*

Smith. Much longer and more detailed than any of the existing amendments, Jefferson's draft addressed the central issue in the first sentence: "The province of Louisiana is incorporated with the U.S. and made part thereof." The remainder unfolded his plan to prevent the early settlement of Louisiana by making it a new homeland for eastern Native Americans. Madison and Smith offered briefer alternate proposals, which suggest that each accepted Jefferson's argument of January that an amendment was "expedient," if not necessary. But Jefferson's own position had changed. Probably as a result of the immensity of the actual purchase, Jefferson apparently decided in July that an amendment was, in fact, needed. "The general government has no powers but such as the constitution has given it," he reminded John Dickinson, "and it has not given it a power of holding foreign territory, & still less of incorporating it into the Union." As such, "an amendment of the Constitution seem[ed] necessary." Jefferson realized that an amendment could not be adopted by Congress and ratified by three-fourths of the states within the six months allotted for approving the treaty. Instead, he believed that Congress should ratify the treaty and then "rely on the nation to sanction an act done for its great good, without its previous authority." With the main point settled, the president and the cabinet members left Washington for the rest of the summer.[71]

Jefferson continued to think about Louisiana, in general, and the constitutional question, in particular, at his mountain home, Monticello, near Charlottesville, Virginia. He devoted his "spare moments to investigat[ing] … the subject of the limits of Louisiana." Using his extensive library, he researched the province's boundaries in histories and treaties, ultimately preparing a brief manuscript that he would later make available for the use of American negotiators. He read the latest dispatches from Europe, which were regularly forwarded to him either directly by State Department clerks or indirectly through Madison, whose own home, Montpelier, was in nearby Orange County, Virginia. He continued his own correspondence on the subject with friends and supporters around the country. And he discussed Louisiana and the constitutional issue with important Republican visitors to Monticello.[72]

During his two-month stay at Monticello, from late July to late September, Jefferson's thinking about an amendment changed not once, but twice. It changed first in response to worrisome reports from Livingston that suggested that Napoleon, as early as late May, had grown dissatisfied with the treaty. *"If he could conveniently get off,"* Livingston warned in a private letter that reached Monticello in mid-August, *"he would." "The slightest pretence [would] be seized to undo the work."* Jefferson could read only a part of this letter when he first received it since he did not have a key to Livingston's cipher at Monticello. What he could read, however, sufficed to convince him "that the less we say about constitutional difficulties respecting Louisiana[,] the better." Jefferson had not suddenly decided that the incorporation of Louisiana was constitutional. But the prospect of losing the treaty through delay or alteration convinced him, as he wrote Madison the day after receiving Livingston's warning, that whatever was needed to overcome the constitutional problems had to "be done sub silentio." "Sub silentio" instantly became Jefferson's favorite phrase. In the first week after receiving Livingston's letter, he used it (or the translation, "in silence") in letters to Thomas Paine, John Breckinridge, Levi Lincoln, and others. He had earlier written to each of these men about the need for an amendment; in mid-August, he wrote back to ask that his initial thoughts on the matter be kept "confidential." That he still thought an amendment necessary, however, is clear. In late August, he sent Madison, Gallatin, and Lincoln a new draft amendment that pared down his original, but still prohibited settlement in almost all of the purchase beyond the Mississippi.[73]

Within ten days, Jefferson had changed his mind again. This time, he reacted to domestic, rather than foreign, politics. In early September, Jefferson received a letter from Virginia Senator Wilson Cary Nicholas. A friend and political ally, Nicholas had visited with Jefferson the previous month and heard his thoughts on the necessity of an amendment. Nicholas argued in this letter that the constitutional authority to admit new states was already "as broad as it cou'd well be made." But his central argument was political, not constitutional. If Jefferson let it be known that he considered the treaty unconstitutional, Nicholas warned, it would probably "be rejected by the Senate, and if that shou'd not happen, … great use wou'd be made with the people, of a wilful breach of the constitution." Jefferson's reply flatly rejected Nicholas's constitutional argument and reaffirmed his own support for strict construction. "Let us not make [the Constitution] a blank paper by construction," he insisted. The popularity of the purchase made "the present case" an especially easy one for "set[ting] an example against broad construction"; it seemed unimaginable that two-thirds of each House of Congress and three-fourths of the states would not support an amendment. But Jefferson ended this lengthy defense of his constitutional interpretation by conceding to Nicholas's political concerns: "If … our friends shall think differently" on the necessity of an amendment, "certainly I shall acquiesce with satisfaction."[74]

The constitutional questions about the Louisiana Purchase did not disappear with Jefferson's concession to "our friends"—meaning his and Nicholas's Republican allies in Congress. Over the course of the ensuing congressional session, they were raised again and again, usually by Federalists. But Jefferson remained not only silent, but inactive. Diplomatic concerns insured that he would say nothing about constitutional matters in his public message. But there is no evidence that he pressed for an amendment even in private correspondence or personal meetings. Perhaps Jefferson ultimately recognized that the Constitution provided no role for the president in the amendment process. An amendment can begin in Congress or in the states. But it cannot be initiated, and does not have to be approved, by the president. In a sense, strict constructionism required Jefferson's silence just as much as he thought it demanded congressional action.

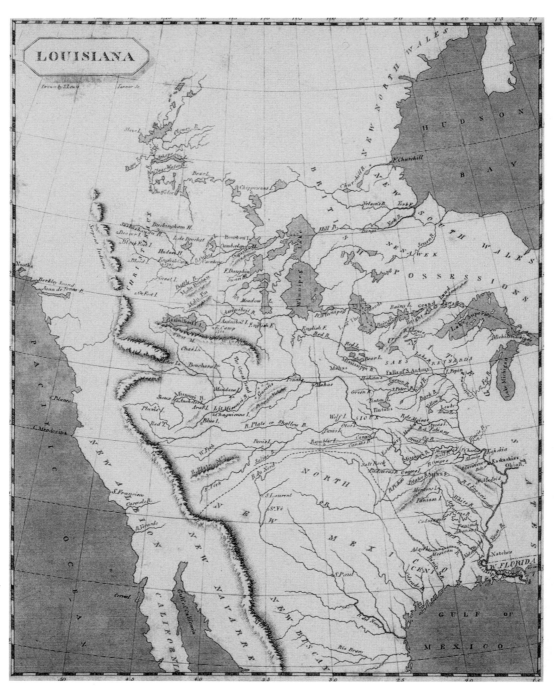

Samuel Lewis's "Map of Louisiana, 1804." (Courtesy Gilcrease Museum, Tulsa, Oklahoma)

Chapter Ten

'This New, Immense, Unbounded World'

"Louisiana ... is of itself a *world*," William Plumer, a New Hampshire Federalist, remarked in his diary on the day that the Senate voted to ratify the treaty. As such, it is not surprising that the Louisiana Purchase created problems and opportunities that often recalled those generated by American independence. What were the boundaries of this "world"? How would it interact with its neighbors, including the United States itself? How would it be governed? Would it be opened or closed to slavery? Having purchased "this new, immense, unbounded world," as another Federalist senator described Louisiana, it became the federal government's responsibility to address these questions. Between early July 1803, when the first news of the treaty reached the United States, and late March 1804, when the next congressional session ended, the administration and Congress began to recognize the problems and opportunities and to answer these fundamental questions.[75]

Not all of the problems created by the treaty were of this magnitude. Some problems were fairly short-lived. For example, Gallatin regretted the specific payment terms that Livingston and Monroe accepted in Paris, believing that they would produce unnecessary expense and confusion. Even some of the most persistent problems were fairly minor. The dispute over the preferential privileges granted to French merchants in Louisiana continued to bedevil Franco-American diplomacy for decades, but never really threatened to produce a rupture between the two countries. The claims convention—under which American merchants were to receive reimbursement for French seizures in the 1790s—generated so much confusion and controversy that some claims were still unresolved nearly a century later. Throughout, however, it was only the claimants and the courts who directly experienced this problem.

A more troubling, though relatively short-lived and still relatively minor, problem was Spain's insistence that the treaty between the United States and France was invalid. Soon after the first news reached Madrid, the Spanish foreign minister informed Pinckney that the Treaty of San Ildefonso had included a secret article in which France agreed never to cede or sell Louisiana to another power without first offering to return it to Spain. When Pinckney and Madison rebuffed this argument, the Spanish foreign minister in Madrid and his representative in Washington countered with a new tactic. France's own claim to Louisiana was invalid, they claimed, because it had never fulfilled its obligation under the Treaty of San Ildefonso to have a Spanish prince recognized as the King of Etruria. Justice was certainly on Spain's side, but Spain lacked the ability to compel just treatment from either nation. "Against such neighbors as France there, and the United States here," Jefferson remarked, Spain's resistance was mere "folly." In his thinking, Spanish opposition to the transfer was never more than "a little cloud hover[ing] in the horizon." In the end, Spain transferred Louisiana to France in late November 1803 without incident, making it possible for the French prefect in New Orleans to transfer it to the American representatives three weeks later.[76]

The most significant diplomatic problem generated by the treaty concerned the boundaries of Louisiana. Livingston and Monroe had wanted to include an explicit statement of the boundaries of the purchase in the treaty. Precisely what was encompassed within the retrocession had been disputed by Spain and France, however. It probably did not extend to both of the Floridas; but did it include any of West Florida? If it did, was the correct boundary between the retroceded territory and Spanish Florida the Pearl River (the modern boundary between Louisiana and the Mississippi panhandle), the Perdido River (the modern boundary between the Alabama and Florida panhandles), or some other line? Equally unclear was the boundary in the West. There was little doubt that Louisiana included the whole western half of the Mississippi watershed. But that definition gave the huge province no frontage on the Gulf Coast west of the river's delta. Clearly, French claims before 1763 had extended along the coast, but how far? Did they reach as far as the Sabine River (the modern divide between Louisiana and

Texas) or to one of the rivers in the modern state of Texas that empty into the Gulf or even all of the way to the Rio Grande? Even after the treaty was signed, Livingston and Monroe tried to have Talleyrand commit himself on the boundaries by asking him what France had expected to receive from Spain. "I can give you no direction," Talleyrand replied, "you have made a noble bargain for yourselves & I suppose you will make the most of it."[77]

Talleyrand captured the essence of the situation. If the undefined boundaries of the cession were a problem for the United States, they were also an opportunity. The greater concern was the eastern border, at least initially. The administration had wanted West Florida even when it had not wanted Louisiana. West Florida still seemed important for the security of American trade on the Mississippi. From the American perspective, the further east Louisiana's boundary could be pushed, the better. If it extended to the Perdido, most of the rivers that flowed into the Gulf from the Mississippi Territory would come entirely under American control. On first reading the treaty, the cabinet believed that it included neither of the Floridas and decided to send Monroe to Madrid "to endeavor to purchase both or

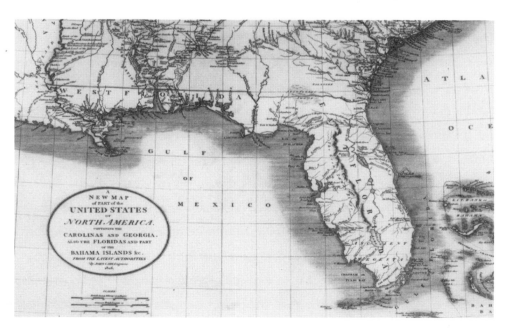

Detail from "A new map of part of the United States of North America, containing the Carolinas and Georgia" (1806) by John Cary. (Courtesy Hargrett Rare Book and Manuscript Library, University of Georgia Libraries)

either" of them. Madison's instructions left no doubt of the continued importance of the Floridas and, thus, of the significance of this problem. He directed Monroe to issue what was at best a barely concealed threat: *"The United States can never* consider the *amicable relations between Spain and them as definitively and permanently secured without an* arrangement on this subject." Madison clearly hoped to intimidate Spain into a sale. But he also saw that, as long as the Floridas remained in Spanish hands, it really would be impossible for Americans to consider their southern frontier secure and peaceful.[78]

If the indefinite language of the treaty did not explicitly *include* West Florida, however, it did not explicitly *exclude* the badly wanted province either. Very quickly, first Livingston and Monroe and later Jefferson, Madison, and Gallatin revisited their early assumption that the purchase did not cover West Florida. In Paris, in Washington, and at Monticello, they investigated the history of French and Spanish exploration and colonization along the Gulf Coast in an attempt to establish the broadest possible American claim. By early June, Livingston and Monroe determined that it was "incontrovertible that W. Florida [was] comprised in the Cession." Jefferson and Gallatin arrived at a similar conclusion by late August. "I was of a different opinion," the latter admitted, "but am now convinced." But satisfying themselves was hardly the same thing as convincing Spain. If the historical evidence did not suffice to persuade Spain to give up West Florida (and it did not), another option for acquiring both of the Floridas was afforded by the indefinite western boundary of the purchase. In Jefferson's opinion, the United States had a solid claim west of Galveston Bay and "some claims" as far as the Rio Grande. Claims along the western Gulf Coast, however weak, could be offered in exchange for the Floridas, without giving Spain any right to use the Mississippi. Madison recognized this possibility almost immediately. An *"adjustment of a boundary between Louisiana and the Spanish territories"* to the west, he suggested to Monroe, might be "combin[ed] with a *cession of the Floridas."* But other priorities took Monroe to London rather than Madrid in the summer of 1803, postponing even the opening of negotiations with Spain on boundary issues.[79]

Finding opportunities in problems became a hallmark of the government's approach to Louisiana between the summer of 1803 and the spring of 1804. One of the most significant problems, in the thinking of many Americans, was the almost magnetic attraction of Louisiana lands for American farmers. Federalists often warned that rapid settlement of the new purchase would depopulate the eastern, particularly New England, states. Farmers who might have bought land in northern New England or upstate New York—much of which was owned by Federalist speculators—would instead move across the river to the milder climate and cheaper lands of the Louisiana Purchase. The political weight of the Federalist-dominated states would be decimated. Decreased populations would mean fewer seats in the House of Representatives; the addition of two senators for each new state from beyond the Mississippi would dilute Federalist influence in the upper house. The finances of Federalist land speculators and the fortunes of the Federalist party did not really concern most Republicans. But Republicans, for the most part, did share the Federalists' deeper fears about the dangers of unchecked settlement in Louisiana. Federalists and Republicans agreed that, if settled too quickly, Louisiana would probably break from the American union, perhaps taking the trans-Appalachian West with it, erect a separate confederation, and become a dangerous neighbor. By the end of August, Jefferson believed that there was "but one opinion as to the necessity of shutting up the country for some time."[80]

Almost immediately, Jefferson saw how the vast expanses of Louisiana could be viewed as an opportunity rather than just a problem. Within a day or two of learning of the treaty, he devised what seemed to be an elegant solution for a number of problems—the threat of an independent Louisiana, the difficulty of governing a distant and dispersed population, and the opposition of the native peoples of the trans-Appalachian West to further land sales. Properly "dispose[d] of," Jefferson argued, Louisiana could become "the means of tempting all our Indians on the east side of the Mississippi to remove to the west, and of condensing instead of scattering our population." He hoped to ban white settlement in almost all of the purchase—he first suggested north of the 31st Parallel and later everything except the modern state of Louisiana—by constitutional amendment or, at least, by law. The few thousand whites who already lived in this region would be forced to relocate. Once west of the Mississippi, the Indians would perform a function that the president would have been uncomfortable assigning to the army, acting as "a Maréchaussée [a rural police force] to prevent emigrants crossing the river." Jefferson believed that this solution would suffice "for half a century," "until we shall have filled up all the vacant country on this side." Once that happened, the government would "lay off a range of States, on the western bank [of the Mississippi] from the head to the mouth," and would remove the Indians further beyond the river. "And so," Jefferson explained, projecting far into the future, "range after range, advancing compactly as we multiply."[81]

Explained again and again by Jefferson in conversations and letters, this plan became widely known as "a favorite measure of the President's." Most Federalists considered it absurd. The settlement of Louisiana could not be prevented or even slowed by law, they insisted. One Federalist senator dismissed as "impracticable" the idea "of removing the [eastern] Indians ... to the western banks of the Mississippi, and of making the fertile regions of Louisiana a howling wilderness, never to be trodden by the foot of civilized man." But it was not just Federalists who questioned Jefferson's plan. The earlier consensus on "shutting up the country" had disappeared by early December, when the president reported "a great division of our friends" in Congress. Some were for barring settlement by constitutional amendment; some were for doing so by law only. "A third set," however, favored "permitting immediate settlement." Even when they hoped to prevent settlement, many western Republicans agreed with the Federalists that any prohibition—by amendment or by law—would prove useless. "You had as well pretend to inhibit the fish from swimming in the sea," Tennessee's William Cocke argued on the Senate floor, "as to prevent the population of that country." In the end, Congress barely considered Jefferson's plan. But Congress's failure to act did not prevent Jefferson from pursuing his goal of preventing white settlement in most of Louisiana; it merely forced him to work through the territorial government and the land office.[82]

One of the valuable effects of making upper Louisiana into an Indian homeland, in Jefferson's mind, was that it would make it unnecessary to organize a government for that vast region for decades. Devising one for what he described as "the inhabited part of Louisiana" seemed problematic enough. Once again, Republicans and Federalists could agree on the central problem. "It is ackonleged,"

Jefferson remarked to a New York Republican, "that our new fellow citizens are as yet as incapable of self government as children." The more settled part of Louisiana included an incredibly heterogeneous population—French and French creole, Spanish and Spanish creole, German, English, and American immigrants, refugees from Acadia and Saint Domingue, Native American, free people of color, and African slaves. It was, according to Massachusetts Federalist Fisher Ames, a *"Gallo-Hispano-Indian omnium gatherum* of savages and adventurers." How could such a population be incorporated into the union or permitted to govern itself? Most Louisianans had no experience with popular government and no familiarity with English legal principles. Few spoke or read English; many were illiterate even in their own language. Most Federalists and many Republicans thought that it would take years to overcome these limitations.[83]

A solution to the problem of government could not be delayed long, however. Some decisions had to be made immediately, so that someone could take charge when France formally transferred Louisiana to the United States. Given the slowness of the mails to the southwestern frontier, Congress had very little time to craft even "temporary provisions" between the ratification of the treaty and the transfer of the province. But something was needed to preserve "order and tranquillity in the country," as Jefferson put it, after the transfer. Within two weeks of the ratification of the treaty, Congress enacted a temporary government law for Louisiana that reflected the need for haste and a desire for order. Republican principles had little place in this law. It allowed for the continuation of existing ordinances and legal practices, granting the president, or his representatives, the arbitrary power of a Spanish governor. It also gave the president complete control over appointing and removing all of the province's officials, including its judges. Through this act, as one Federalist complained, the president was "made as despotic as the Grand Turk."[84]

A critical early decision, therefore, concerned the proper governor for the new province. Writing to Madison to offer himself for the post, Monroe explained as well as anyone why it was so important to choose the right man. "Sound principles" needed to "be established there in the outset, to bind the new acquired territory & people to the union." "At the head of a population so mixed [and] with so many objects to allure an ambitious & rapacious mind," "a man of loose principles" would be capable of anything. Jefferson would not have disagreed with this assessment. But he also suggested more specific criteria for the position in a late July letter to Madison proposing South Carolina's Thomas Sumter. The characteristics that made Sumter "as perfect in all points as we can expect," in Jefferson's view, included: "sound judgment, standing in society, knolege of the world, wealth, liberality, familiarity with the French language, & having a French wife." The man that the administration ultimately, and begrudgingly, accepted for the position could boast few of these traits. Few people—Federalist or Republican, within the administration or without—considered William C. C. Claiborne, the young governor of the Mississippi Territory, the right man for the job. "Loose principles," in Monroe's words, were not the problem. But "neither his manners, disposition, or talents qualif[ied]" Claiborne for the position; "the simple circumstance of his ignorance of the French language & manners [was] no small objection." It took years before Claiborne, who ultimately governed Louisiana as territory and state until 1816, convinced even his administration friends that he was competent to the task.[85]

Forming a temporary government and choosing a governor for Louisiana were just the first steps in addressing the problem of government for the new acquisition. During the summer, Jefferson seemed to suggest, in various letters, that the next step would be easy. The settled part of Louisiana, he wrote Breckinridge, must "of course be immediately a territorial government, and soon a State." In 1787, the Northwest Ordinance had established a system for territorial governance and new state formation that included a three-stage process. First, each territory would be governed by an appointed governor, secretary, and judges. Once its population reached five thousand free, adult males, it could establish a legislature with a popularly elected lower house and send a nonvoting delegate to Congress. When its population reached sixty thousand free inhabitants, the territory could be admitted to the union. But Jefferson eventually decided that such a government would "not do at all" in lower Louisiana; "it would turn all their laws topsyturvy." With a population of around fifty thousand, Louisiana should have started with a second-stage territorial government, enjoyed substantial local self-rule, and been able to look forward to statehood in just a few years. But Jefferson wanted

Louisianans to begin with a first-stage government and proceed through a far more gradual process in which "their laws & organisation" would be conformed "to the mould of ours by degrees as they find practicable without exciting too much discontent." Instead of the three-stage process of the Northwest Ordinance, Jefferson projected frequent congressional action. "From session to session," Congress would extend rights and responsibilities in Louisiana "in proportion as [it found] the people there ripen[ed] for receiving" them.[86]

Jefferson's views shaped the Louisiana government bill that Congress debated during the first three months of 1804. In fact, Jefferson drafted the so-called "Breckinridge bill" that was the subject of these debates. Finding Breckinridge, the chair of the Senate committee that was to draft the bill, stymied by the task, Jefferson sent him his own proposal "in confidence." Minor revisions were all that differentiated Jefferson's draft of late November from the bill that Breckinridge's committee reported in late December. Jefferson's proposal provided for local, but not popular, government in the form of an "Assembly of Notables"—a group of twenty-four local property-owners who would be appointed by the governor. This assembly would act as a legislature and would be limited only by the provision that its laws could not violate the federal Constitution. Jefferson's draft also called for a court system in which English legal practices and rights, including that to trial by jury, would be gradually incorporated "as the habits and state of the peoples of the territory [would] admit." Breckinridge replaced "Assembly of Notables" with "legislative council" and made a few other changes, but otherwise left Jefferson's plan intact.[87]

Devising a long-term government for Louisiana proved incredibly difficult and divisive, even with a strong Republican majority in each house of Congress. The views expressed in Congress covered an amazingly broad spectrum. At one extreme, many Federalists argued that Louisiana should be governed "as a colony," with no expectation that it would ever become an equal member of the union. At the other, John Quincy Adams, a Federalist senator from Massachusetts, insisted that Congress would violate the fundamental principle of American independence—the consent of the governed—if it adopted any form of government for Louisiana without first obtaining "the express consent of the inhabitants thereof."

Republicans expressed a breadth of views, as well. Though none went as far as Adams, many Republicans also recoiled from "suspend[ing the] principles [of self-government] for a single moment." Others agreed with Jefferson that Louisiana formed a special case, to which the established territorial system could not be applied. Louisiana needed "an original system, founded on new principles," according to one. Its government would be "unlike anything in Heaven, in earth or under it." After months of debate, Congress passed an act of governance for the purchase in late March 1804. The provisions for Louisiana south of the 33rd Parallel (confusingly renamed Orleans Territory) differed little from those prepared by Jefferson and proposed by Breckinridge. Upper Louisiana was, at least temporarily, made a district of the Indiana Territory.[88]

Jefferson's solution to the problem of governing Louisiana may have deviated further from republican principles than many of his supporters liked, but his appraisal of the opportunities for republicanism opened by the purchase must have restored their confidence. Even as he confessed his uncertainty about whether Louisiana would finally remain in the American union, Jefferson insisted that it would be republican. "The world will here see such an extent of country under a free and moderate government," he wrote Tennessee's Andrew Jackson in September 1803, "as it has never yet seen." The difficulties of arranging a territorial government for Louisiana did not dampen his enthusiasm or his optimism. In late January, at a time when even the Republicans in Congress had splintered over the Louisiana government bill, Jefferson boasted of the "duplication of area for the extending a government so free and economical as ours … as a great achievement." Within the next two years, he began to apply to the Louisiana Purchase a phrase that he had used for the trans-Appalachian West a quarter of a century earlier: the "empire of liberty." This phrase, or the variant "empire for liberty," came to characterize his view of American expansion. He returned to it throughout his life as a shorthand for the spread of American-style republican governments across the North American continent. Less than two months into his retirement, Jefferson assured his successor, Madison, that "no constitution was ever before so well calculated as ours for extensive empire and self-government."[89]

Could slavery have a place in an "empire of liberty"? The Louisiana Purchase reopened this fundamental question—one which had arisen when the confederation government began to prepare for the settlement of the trans-Appalachian West in the early 1780s. In March 1784, Jefferson had drafted a plan of government that would have prohibited slavery in all of the states west of the Appalachians, north and south of the Ohio River, after 1800. But Congress rejected this clause. When it adopted the Northwest Ordinance three years later, it prohibited slavery without the fifteen-year delay of Jefferson's plan, but only for the region north of the Ohio. Two decades later, Jefferson's ideas about the settlement and government of Louisiana had important implications for the future of slavery in the West (now the trans-Mississippi West). His plan to empty upper Louisiana of its white settlers and refill it with the eastern Indians would have postponed a decision about whether to permit the expansion of slavery for a generation or more. In this matter, as in so many others, Jefferson probably thought, as he remarked in a slightly different context, that "we [could] safely trust the provisions for that time to the men who shall live in it."[90]

A similar postponement was not possible for lower Louisiana, however. There, slaves formed a large part of the population and were deeply entrenched in the economic and social systems. What Jefferson proposed—in a memorandum that he sent to Gallatin in November 1803 with the intention that Gallatin would convey its contents to Republican congressmen—was closing lower Louisiana to the importation of additional slaves "except from such of the [states] as prohibit importation" from abroad. None of his other writings from this period explain his thinking more fully. One thing is clear, though. Jefferson did not expect to end, or even to limit, slavery in lower Louisiana through this step. In November 1803, no state permitted the importation of slaves from abroad, though Jefferson may have known that a movement to reopen the trade was gaining strength in South Carolina. Louisianans—present and future—would have been able to purchase slaves from any other state that permitted slavery, as well as from northern states whose gradual emancipation laws allowed slave-owners to sell their human property out of state. But, if Jefferson's plan had no real anti-slavery implications for Louisiana, it may have had some, in his thinking, for states like Delaware, Maryland, and Virginia. The demand for slaves in Louisiana—a demand that could not have been met from abroad—would have been met primarily with slaves from the upper South, making it easier for those states to end slavery within their borders. Years later, as the country divided over whether or not to permit slavery in Missouri, Jefferson spoke of this process as one of "diffusion." In 1803, he may have already believed that the problem of slavery *in* Louisiana was also an opportunity to end slavery *outside* Louisiana.[91]

What to do about slavery in Louisiana emerged as perhaps the most divisive question as the Senate debated the government bill. To John Quincy Adams, the struggle over this question was as slow and painful as "the drawing of a jaw tooth." Some senators, particularly northern Federalists, hoped to adopt a measure that would end slavery throughout the purchase. Others, especially southern Republicans, opposed any limitation on slavery, at least in lower Louisiana. But most senators—northern and southern, Federalist and Republican—sought some limit on the introduction of additional slaves into the territory. Jefferson's suggestion of prohibiting the importation of any slaves into Louisiana from outside of the United States—whether directly from overseas or indirectly through South Carolina, which reopened its trade in early 1804—was one possibility. Others would have broadened or narrowed the classes of slaves to be excluded. No plan seemed capable of "reconcil[ing] the two parties of slave and anti-slave into which the *majority* [were] divided," Adams reported. The slavery provisions of the final act emerged from an amendment process in which some proposals were defeated and others were approved—sometimes by broad and sometimes by narrow margins. In the end, the act permitted the introduction of slaves into lower Louisiana only with a "bona fide owner" who was moving into the "territory for actual settlement." In upper Louisiana, the act prohibited slavery entirely, but only temporarily, by placing the region under the government of the Indiana Territory, where slavery was banned by the Northwest Ordinance. However limited, these restrictions instantly produced dissatisfaction throughout Louisiana; within just a couple of years, lower Louisiana emerged as a major market for slaves imported through South Carolina.[92]

The fundamental questions raised by the Louisiana Purchase—questions about boundaries, settlement, government, and slavery—had been addressed in some form when Congress adjourned in late March 1804. But few people—whether in the administration, in Congress, or in the newly acquired territory—believed that they had been answered in full. It would take the Transcontinenal Treaty of 1819 to resolve the boundary dispute. That resolution ultimately took the form that Jefferson and Madison had seen in 1803—an exchange of American claims to Texas for Spanish claims to the Floridas. No meaningful limits were ever placed on white settlement beyond the Mississippi; when President Andrew Jackson pressed Indian removal in the 1830s, he did not share Jefferson's goal. It was not until the mid-1820s, following a resurgence of western separatism at the beginning of the decade, that most Americans felt confident that the trans-Mississippi West would remain in the union. The governance of the Orleans Territory sparked local controversy and national debate for nearly a decade; only in 1812, largely in response to a looming war with Great Britain, did Louisiana become a state. Elsewhere in the purchase, however, the regular process of territorial government and state formation smoothly added new areas to Jefferson's "empire of liberty." The most intractable problem created by the Louisiana Purchase proved to be the slavery question. Temporary solutions were reached in the Missouri Compromise (1820), in the Compromise of 1850, and in the Kansas-Nebraska Act (1854); but it was the inability of the political system to handle the question of slavery in the trans-Mississippi West, as much as any other single issue, that led to the Civil War.

Velvet silk cover of the French exchange copy of one of the conventions that comprise the Louisiana Purchase. (Courtesy National Archives)

Chapter Eleven

WASHINGTON, JANUARY 1804

On January 15, 1804, news reached the nation's capital that Louisiana had been officially and "amicably surrendered to the United States" by France at a ceremony in New Orleans nearly a month earlier. To commemorate the transfer, congressional Republicans threw a pair of parties that were intended to serve as an "example" for Americans everywhere, "who appreciate[d], as highly as their representatives, this great event." On January 27, "a numerous company assembled at Stelle's Hotel, on Capitol Hill," for "a most superb dinner." The guests included the president and vice president, the department heads, other government officials, and many of the members of Congress. The president was escorted to the hotel by various civil and military officials, "announced by a discharge of artillery," "and welcomed by a full band of music playing 'Jefferson's March.'" Four days later, the party moved to Georgetown, where the Republican members of Congress held a ball that *The National Intelligencer,* a paper friendly to the administration, described as "by far the most numerous and brilliant" yet held in the capital. The walls were festooned with laurel; there was "a transparent portrait of the President" at one end of the hall surrounded by the banners of the military corps; and all of "the windows of the House were illuminated"—an effect enhanced by the reflection of the light in the snow. "About 200 Ladies, and near 300 Gentlemen" attended the ball. Despite the size of the crowd, according to the paper, "the most perfect good order, and the highest flow of hilarity," were maintained. The editor admitted that the plain buildings "and the still plainer equality of our manners" might make a poor spectacle to "foreign eye[s]" and "foreign habits." But "the extention of the empire of freedom, and of peace," was so worthy of celebration as to "put place and form out of consideration."[93]

Federalists viewed these events quite differently. "Two days are to be devoted here to Democratic hilarity," Manasseh Cutler reported: "One to *eating* and *drinking*, and the other to *fiddling and dancing.*" Only those Federalists who actually supported the purchase attended the dinner. John Quincy Adams went, but left "at eight in the evening," recording in his diary that "the dinner was bad, and the toasts too numerous." In those hard-drinking days, it was standard at public celebrations to drink one toast per state—seventeen with the recent addition of Ohio—in addition to "volunteers." "A number of the guests drank so many toasts," one Federalist diarist noted, "that in the night they returned to their houses without their hats." More Federalists attended the ball in Georgetown. But their accounts of it shared the same disparaging tone. According to Adams, "the arrangements and decorations were mean beyond any thing of the kind I ever saw." Federalists, who typically believed that a government needed a little pomp to inspire and awe the people, considered the whole "Jubilee" on the acquisition of Louisiana to be "a very trifling matter." There was a dinner and a ball; and "three or four cannon were fired." But "there was no parade nor coll[a]tions among the people," one Federalist reported in disgust.[94]

The differences between Republicans and Federalists over the "jubilee" were only partially a reflection of their often-conflicting views on the propriety of official celebrations and spectacles in a republican government, however. Three months after the ratification of the treaty, the two parties were still bitterly divided over the Louisiana Purchase itself. An anonymous essayist in the city's Federalist paper, *The Washington Federalist*, responded to the celebrations with a lengthy attack on the administration and the treaty. The Republicans sought "to claim a laurel" when they "deserved impeachment." An "accidental event," the treaty benefitted Napoleon far more than the United States. Rather than "securing what we really required [New Orleans]," it shackled us with "a country at least two thousand miles from us, peopled by a motley race of vagabonds, who are to be our citizens." In ratifying it, the Republicans had "gone far beyond the constitutional limits." And for what end, the essayist wondered? Louisiana would lure farmers from the East; in time, they would raise so much cotton and tobacco that these articles would become "a mere drug" on the market. Even more worrisome were its "inevitable" effects on the union. The accession of so many new states beyond the Mississippi would surely drive the eastern states to secede. "Such an event would be deplorable"; but the alternative would be even "more fatal." Louisiana was so vast and so distant that it would soon become independent, forming "a numerous and dangerous power" "on our frontier." "If such a series of misfortunes and national calamities" was considered "a subject worthy of joy and celebration," the essayist concluded, "posterity [would] blush for [the public's] ignorance and delusion."[95]

Republicans, in contrast, saw good cause to celebrate. As the editor of *The National Intelligencer* put it, "they had acquired almost a new world, and had laid the foundation for the happiness of millions yet unborn!" And they had done so "by means unstained with the blood of a single victim." Accounts of celebratory dinners and balls poured into Washington from across the country for weeks. Orations and toasts cheered republican government, peaceful negotiations, and future expansion, while condemning the Federalists for advocating war, criticizing the purchase, and denigrating "our brethren of Louisiana." But many of these toasts also hinted at some of the same concerns that troubled Federalists. At a dinner in Alexandria, Virginia, for example, celebrants drank to "the citizens of America on both sides of the Mississippi," hoping that "one interest [might] rivet the union we this day celebrate." Republicans in Lexington, Kentucky, hoped that "the citizens of Louisiana" would "be loyal to the government … [and] properly appreciate the blessings of republicanism."[96]

In the days between the dinner and ball, both of which he attended, Jefferson reflected on the defining event of his first term as president—the crisis over Louisiana—in a letter to the English immigrant Joseph Priestley. "I very early saw that Louisiana was indeed a speck on the horizon which was to burst into a tornado," Jefferson stated. He insisted that "nothing but a frank and friendly development of causes and effects on our part, and good sense enough in Bonaparte," had "saved us from that storm." It had only been necessary to wait until a new war between France and Great Britain, and to prevent Federalist hot-heads from "forc[ing] a premature rupture," to end the crisis. There had been risks in such a plan, Jefferson admitted. But "the *dénouement* [had] been happy." The Louisiana

Purchase had doubled the size of the United States. And, even if the trans-Mississippi West did not remain in the union, Jefferson trusted that it would be populated by "our children and descendants" and governed by similar institutions.[97]

Jefferson's letters to Priestley, like those to most of his "enlightened" European correspondents, typically offered the most favorable and optimistic assessments. But self-criticism was never one of his strengths. Others, at the time and since, found much to criticize in Jefferson's handling of the Mississippi crisis. We might readily agree with these critics that the fact that the crisis ended in the Louisiana Purchase—and not the "New Orleans Purchase" or the "West Florida Purchase"—stemmed more from the European war and the Saint Domingue rebellion than from American policymaking. But that it ended in a treaty at all, rather than in a war with France or an alliance with Great Britain, must be credited to Jefferson's, and the administration's, refusal to adopt the course advocated by the Federalists. Jefferson and his cabinet understood that the real threat of the retrocession of Louisiana was to the union of the states. As such, they rejected any measure, including immediate war with France or entangling alliance with Great Britain, that seemed more dangerous to the union than a weak French colony in Louisiana. Only a French effort to control the economic prospects, and thus the political loyalties, of the trans-Appalachian West justified an immediate rupture in their eyes.

If the criticism of Jefferson's policymaking has continued, the attacks on its results—the acquisition of all of Louisiana—has not. Within just a few years, the purchase's overwhelming domestic popularity silenced even the most violent Federalists; their views have never been revived. Developments in Louisiana over the course of the nineteenth century fit much better with Jefferson's dreams of an expanding "empire of liberty" than the Federalists' fears of a divided union and hostile neighborhood. But Jefferson's dreams, as expansive as they were in terms of geography, were always limited in terms of race. Federalists recognized this limitation even at the time. "*Louisiana* is to be a field of blood before it is a cultivated field," one Federalist essayist warned, "and indeed a field of blood while it is cultivated." Jefferson's "extension of human liberty and of human happiness" would necessitate the violent dispossession of "the natives of the soil" and the equally violent importation of African slaves "to toil and bleed under the lash." The story of the trans-Mississippi West in the nineteenth century included *both* the expansion of republican government and formation of new states *and* the destruction of Native American nations and oppression of African-American slaves.[98]

Suggested Readings

The Louisiana Purchase has fascinated scholars since the earliest days of academic history in the United States. Every generation seems to produce a classic account, many of which remain useful for scholars and informative for general readers.

All students of Jefferson's presidency should spend at least some time with Henry Adams's monumental *History of the United States of America during the Administrations of Thomas Jefferson and James Madison*, 9 vols. (New York: Charles Scribner's Sons, 1889-1891). Adams, the great-grandson of John and grandson of John Quincy, often criticized Jefferson's handling of these events. In the 1930s, two important books shifted the focus away from Washington. E. Wilson Lyon's *Louisiana in French Diplomacy, 1759-1804* (Norman: University of Oklahoma Press, 1934) examined the Louisiana Purchase from the perspective of Paris. Arthur Preston Whitaker's *The Mississippi Question, 1795-1803: A Study in Trade, Politics, and Diplomacy* (New York: D. Appleton-Century Company, Inc., 1934) emphasized developments on the frontier. In the 1970s, Alexander DeConde placed the Louisiana Purchase at the center of an American quest for territorial and commercial empire in *This Affair of Louisiana* (New York: Charles Scribner's Sons, 1976). In the early 1990s, political scientists Robert W. Tucker and David C. Hendrickson revisited and extended Henry Adams's critique of Jeffersonian foreign policy in *Empire of Liberty: The Statecraft of Thomas Jefferson* (New York: Oxford University Press, 1990).

A number of works help to place Louisiana within a broader perspective of American thinking about international systems. My own *The American Union and the Problem of Neighborhood: The United States and the Collapse of the Spanish Empire, 1783-1829* (Chapel Hill: University of North Carolina Press, 1998) concerns hemispheric developments. Peter S. Onuf examines ideas about federal systems in a continental or Atlantic context in: (with Nicholas Onuf) *Federal Union, Modern World: The Law of Nations in an Age of Revolutions, 1776-1814* (Madison, Wisc.:

Madison House, 1993); "The Expanding Union," in David Thomas Konig, ed., *Devising Liberty: Preserving and Creating Freedom in the New American Republic* (Stanford, Calif.: Stanford University Press, 1995), 50-80; and *Jefferson's Empire: The Language of American Nationhood* (Charlottesville: University Press of Virginia, 2000).

The opportunities and problems created by the purchase are discussed in various works. For concerns about expansion, see Michael Allen, "The Federalists and the West, 1783-1803," *Western Pennsylvania Historical Magazine* 61 (October 1978): 315-32; and Reginald Horsman, "The Dimensions of an 'Empire for Liberty': Expansion and Republicanism, 1775-1825," *Journal of the Early Republic* 9 (Spring 1989): 1-20. Tucker and Hendrickson's *Empire of Liberty* covers the diplomatic aftermath, particularly the effort to acquire the Floridas; this subject is also treated in Clifford L. Egan, *Neither Peace Nor War: Franco-American Relations, 1803-1812* (Baton Rouge: Louisiana State University Press, 1983). The many constitutional and governmental questions generated by the purchase are thoroughly canvassed in Everett S. Brown's *The Constitutional History of the Louisiana Purchase, 1803-1812* (Berkeley: University of California Press, 1920). More recent discussions of the constitutionality question include: Barry J. Balleck, "When the Ends Justify the Means: Thomas Jefferson and the Louisiana Purchase," *Presidential Studies Quarterly* 22 (Fall 1992): 679-96; and David P. Currie, "The Constitution in Congress: Jefferson and the West, 1801-1809," *William & Mary Law Review* 39 (May 1998): 1441-1503. The slavery debates are examined at some length in Everett Brown's book. For a recent article that touches on this issue, see Jed Handelsman Shugerman, "The Louisiana Purchase and South Carolina's Reopening of the Slave Trade in 1803," *Journal of the Early Republic* 22 (Summer 2002): 263-90.

Most of the principals in this drama have been the subjects of biographies. The most valuable Jefferson biographies for students of the Louisiana Purchase are Dumas Malone's *Jefferson the President: First Term, 1801-1805*, vol. 4 of *Jefferson and His Time* (Boston: Little, Brown and Company, 1970); and Merrill D. Peterson's *Thomas Jefferson and the New Nation: A Biography* (New York: Oxford University Press, 1970). Lawrence S. Kaplan combines biography and diplomatic history in *Thomas Jefferson: Westward the Course of Empire* (Wilmington, Del.: SR

Books, 1999). Helpful biographies of the other actors in the Louisiana Purchase include: E. Wilson Lyon, *The Man Who Sold Louisiana: The Career of François Barbé-Marbois* (Norman: University of Oklahoma Press, 1942); Irving Brant, *James Madison: Secretary of State, 1800-1809*, vol. 4 of *James Madison* (Indianapolis, Ind.: Bobbs-Merrill Company, Inc., 1953); George Dangerfield, *Chancellor Robert R. Livingston of New York, 1746-1813* (New York: Harcourt, Brace, 1960); and Harry Ammon, *James Monroe: The Quest for National Identity* (New York: McGraw-Hill Book Company, 1971).

Useful reference works include: Dolores Egger Labbé, ed., *The Louisiana Purchase and Its Aftermath, 1800-1830*, vol. 3 of *The Louisiana Purchase Bicentennial Series in Louisiana History* (Lafayette: Center for Louisiana Studies, University of Southwestern Louisiana, 1998); and Junius P. Rodriguez, ed., *The Louisiana Purchase: A Historical and Geographical Encyclopedia* (Santa Barbara, Calif.: ABC-Clio, 2002).

With the bicentennial of the Louisiana Purchase certain to spark renewed public and scholarly interest, we will surely see new accounts and interpretations over the next few years. Peter J. Kastor has already provided a glimpse of his forthcoming work on the incorporation of Louisiana into the union in "'Motives of Peculiar Urgency': Local Diplomacy in Louisiana, 1803-1821," *William and Mary Quarterly* 3d ser., 58 (October 2001): 819-48. And Jon Kukla's *A Wilderness So Immense: The Louisiana Purchase and the Destiny of America* (New York: Alfred A. Knopf, Inc., 2003) will be published while this book is at the press.

NOTES

1.   Jefferson to Thomas Mann Randolph, Jr., July 5, 1803, Thomas Jefferson Papers, on-line edition, Library of Congress, Washington, D.C. (hereafter LC: Jefferson Papers). I exercise a bit of artistic license in dating the shock of "all Louisiana" to early July. This letter seems to be Jefferson's first mention of the treaty. But, from other letters, it is clear that the cabinet knew by mid- to late June that Livingston and Monroe had received a proposal to buy the whole province. Of course, the information was no less startling then.

2.   Livingston and Monroe to Madison, May 13, 1803, Robert J. Brugger, et al., eds., *The Papers of James Madison: Secretary of State Series*, 6 vols. to date (Charlottesville: University Press of Virginia, 1986—), 4:601 (hereafter *Madison Papers (SSS)*); Monroe to Madison, May 14, 1803, ibid., 610; Jefferson to Madison, July 17, 1803, ibid., 5:191.

3.   Madison to Monroe, June 25, 1803, ibid., 117. Italicized words were originally in code.

4.   Ibid., 118; Monroe to Madison, May 14, 1803, ibid., 4:610; Jefferson to DuPont de Nemours, November 1, 1803, Andrew A. Lipscomb and Albert Ellery Bergh, eds., *The Writings of Thomas Jefferson*, Definitive Edition, 20 vols. (Washington, D.C.: Thomas Jefferson Memorial Association, 1905-1907), 10:423 (hereafter *Jefferson Writings*). Jefferson discussed his plan with Meriwether Lewis before the latter left Washington for Pittsburgh, and beyond, on July 5. Italicized words were originally in code.

5.   Wistar to Jefferson, July 18 [misfiled as 13], 1803, LC: Jefferson Papers.

6.   Jedidiah Morse, *The American Geography: or A View of the Present Situation of the United States of America* (Elizabethtown, N.J.: Shepard Pollock, 1789), 469.

7.   Jefferson to Archibald Stuart, January 25, 1786, Julian P. Boyd, et al., eds., *The Papers of Thomas Jefferson*, 30 vols. to date (Princeton, N.J.: Princeton University Press, 1950—), 9: 218 (hereafter *Jefferson Papers*); Jefferson to Monroe, November 24, 1801, *Jefferson Writings*, 10:296.

8.   "Publius" [Hamilton], "The Federalist No. 6," Jacob E. Cooke, ed., *The Federalist* (Middletown, Conn.: Wesleyan University Press, 1961), 28.

9.   "Publius" [Hamilton], "The Federalist No. 8," ibid., 49.

10.   Washington to Henry Knox, December 5, 1784, W. W. Abbot, et al., eds., *The Papers of George Washington: Confederation Series*, 6 vols. (Charlottesville: University Press of Virginia, 1992-1997), 2:171.

11.   Madison to Lafayette, March 20, 1785, William T. Hutchinson, et al., eds., *The Papers of James Madison*, 17 vols. (Chicago: University of Chicago Press, 1962-1977; Charlottesville: University Press of Virginia, 1977-1991), 8:250-51 (hereafter *Madison Papers*).

12.   Jefferson to Monroe, July 9, 1786, *Jefferson Papers*, 10:112-13.

13 Madison to Washington, March 18, 1787, *Madison Papers*, 9:316; Monroe to Madison, August 14, 1786, ibid., 104.

14 Jefferson to Monroe, August 11, 1786, *Jefferson Papers*, 10:223; Jefferson to Madison, December 16, 1786, ibid., 603; Jefferson to Madison, June 20, 1787, ibid., 11:481; Jefferson to Madison, December 16, 1786, ibid., 10:603; Jefferson to Monroe, August 11, 1786, ibid., 224. Italicized words were originally in code.

15 Gouverneur Morris to the Princess de la Tour et Taxis, December 14, 1800, Anne Cary Morris, ed., *The Diary and Letters of Gouverneur Morris*, 2 vols. (New York: Charles Scribner's Sons, 1888), 2:395.

16 King to Madison, March 29, 1801, *Madison Papers (SSS)*, 1:55; William Vans Murray to Madison, May 20, 1801, ibid., 206.

17 Jefferson to Thomas Pinckney, May 29, 1797, *Jefferson Papers*, 29:405; "Titus Manlius" [Hamilton], "The Stand No. IV," April 12, 1798, Harold C. Syrett and Jacob E. Cooke, eds., *The Papers of Alexander Hamilton*, 27 vols. (New York: Columbia University Press, 1961-1987), 21:414 (hereafter *Hamilton Papers*); Hamilton to Harrison Gray Otis, January 26, 1799, ibid., 22:441.

18 Jefferson, "Outline of Policy on the Mississippi Question," enclosed in Jefferson to William Carmichael, August 2, 1790, *Jefferson Papers*, 17:115; Edmund Randolph to Jefferson, August 28, 1794, ibid., 28:117-18; Jefferson to Randolph, September 7, 1794, ibid., 148.

19 Madison to Charles Pinckney, June 9, 1801, *Madison Papers (SSS)*, 1:275; Madison to Livingston, July 11, 1801, ibid., 403; Jefferson to Monroe, May 26, 1801, Paul Leicester Ford, ed., *The Works of Thomas Jefferson*, Federal Edition, 12 vols. (New York: G. P. Putnam's Sons, 1904-1905), 9:260 (hereafter *Jefferson Works*).

20 Jefferson to Stuart, January 25, 1786, *Jefferson Papers*, 9:218; Madison to Charles Pinckney, June 9, 1801, *Madison Papers (SSS)*, 1:276; Madison to King, July 24, 1801, ibid., 470.

21 Madison to King, July 24, 1801, ibid., 469-70.

22 Monroe to Madison, June 14, 1801, ibid., 315; Madison to Charles Pinckney, June 9, 1801, ibid., 275. An extract of this letter was included in Livingston's instructions.

23 Madison to Livingston, September 28, 1801, ibid., 2:144; Madison to Charles Pinckney, June 9, 1801, ibid., 1:276; Madison to Livingston, September 28, 1801, ibid., 2:144-45. Madison and Jefferson apparently prepared Livingston's instructions together at the former's plantation, Montpelier.

24 Madison to Livingston, September 28, 1801, ibid., 145.

25 Livingston to Madison, January 13, 1802, ibid., 389; Livingston to Madison, December 31, 1801, ibid., 359. Italicized words were originally in code.

26 Jefferson to Livingston, April 18, 1802, *Jefferson Writings*, 10:311-15.

27 Jefferson to Livingston, May 5, 1802, LC: Jefferson Papers; Jefferson to DuPont, April 25, 1802, *Jefferson Writings*, 10:317. Jefferson later informed Livingston: "*My* letters to you being merely private, I leave all details of business to their official channel" (Jefferson to Livingston, October 10, 1802, ibid., 337).

28 Madison to Livingston, March 16, 1802, *Madison Papers (SSS)*, 3:38. Italicized words were originally in code.

29 DuPont to Jefferson, April 30, 1802, Dumas Malone, ed., *Correspondence between Thomas Jefferson and Pierre Samuel du Pont de Nemours, 1798-1817* (Boston: Houghton Mifflin Company, 1930), 54, 58; Jefferson to Livingston, May 5, 1802, LC: Jefferson Papers; Jefferson to DuPont, May 5, 1802, Papers of DuPont de Nemours, Winterthur Manuscript Group 2, Hagley Museum and Library, Wilmington, Del. (hereafter Hagley: DuPont Papers). I appreciate the assistance of the Papers of Thomas Jefferson Project in tracking down a copy of Jefferson's letter to DuPont.

30 Jefferson to Gallatin, August 20, 1802, Henry Adams, ed., *The Writings of Albert Gallatin*, 3 vols. (Philadelphia: J. B. Lippincott & Co., 1879), 1:93 (hereafter *Gallatin Writings*); Madison to Livingston, October 15, 1802, *Madison Papers (SSS)*, 4:24-25.

31 Jefferson to Livingston, April 18, 1802, *Jefferson Writings*, 10:313; Livingston to Madison, July 30, 1802, *Madison Papers (SSS)*, 3:443; Madison to Livingston, May 1, 1802, ibid., 175-76; Madison to King, May 1, 1802, ibid., 173; Charles Pinckney to Madison, August 24, 1802, ibid., 513.

32 Pichon to Charles-Maurice Talleyrand-Périgord, July 20, 1801, ibid., 1:403 n.1; Madison to Charles Pinckney, May 11, 1802, ibid., 3:215-16; Jefferson to DuPont, May 5, 1802, Hagley: DuPont Papers.

33 Livingston to Madison, April 24, 1802, *Madison Papers (SSS)*, 3:157; Livingston to Madison, August 19, 1802, ibid., 500; Livingston to Madison, September 1, 1802, ibid., 536. Italicized words were originally in code.

34 Unknown letter writer, March 2, 1801, quoted in Arthur Preston Whitaker, *The Mississippi Question, 1795-1803: A Study in Trade, Politics, and Diplomacy* (New York: D. Appleton-Century Company, Inc., 1934), 44; William Johnson, journal entry, [ca. April-May] 1801, quoted in ibid., 43.

35 Unknown letter writer, March 2, 1801, quoted in ibid.

36 Hūlings to Madison, November 25, 1802, *Madison Papers (SSS)*, 4:140.

37 Meeker, Williamson, & Patton to John Brown, October 18, 1802, enclosed in Brown to Jefferson, November 26, 1802, LC: Jefferson Papers; Claiborne to Madison, October 29, 1802, *Madison Papers (SSS)*, 4:67; Memorial of the Kentucky legislature, December 1, 1802, ibid., 179 n.1; Hore Browse Trist to Mary Trist, December 10, 1802, Nicholas P.

Trist Papers, Southern Historical Collection, University of North Carolina, Chapel Hill; Barbour to Madison, December 9, 1802, *Madison Papers (SSS)*, 4:184.

[38] Samuel Johnston to unknown correspondent, March 18, 1803, Hayes Collection, Southern Historical Collection, University of North Carolina, Chapel Hill; Clark to Madison, April 27, 1803, "Despatches from the United States Consulate in New Orleans, 1801-1803," *American Historical Review* 33 (January 1928): 340.

[39] Barry to John Barry, May 9, 1803, William T. Barry letters, Alderman Library, University of Virginia, Charlottesville.

[40] Jefferson to Livingston, April 18, 1802, *Jefferson Writings*, 10:315.

[41] Madison to Charles Pinckney, November 27, 1802, *Madison Papers (SSS)*, 4:147; Jefferson to Madison, August 30, 1802, ibid., 3:527; Madison to King, December 23, 1802, ibid., 4:216.

[42] Jefferson to Dearborn, "Hints on the subject of Indian boundaries, suggested for consideration," December 29, 1802, LC: Jefferson Papers; Jefferson to Claiborne, May 24, 1803, *Jefferson Writings*, 10:391; Jefferson to John Bacon, April 30, 1803, *Jefferson Works*, 9:464; Jefferson to William H. Harrison, February 27, 1803, *Jefferson Writings*, 10:369-70, 373.

[43] Hamilton to Charles Cotesworth Pinckney, December 29, 1802, *Hamilton Papers*, 26:71-72.

[44] Jefferson to Monroe, January 13, 1803, *Jefferson Writings*, 10: 343-44; Jefferson to Livingston, February 3, 1803, ibid., 353.

[45] [Charles Brockden Brown], *Monroe's Embassy, or The Conduct of the Government, in Relation to Our Claims to the Navigation of the Mississippi* (Philadelphia: John Conrad & Co., 1803), quoted in Alexander DeConde, *This Affair of Louisiana* (New York: Charles Scribner's Sons, 1976), 139; "Pericles" [Hamilton], "For the *Evening Post*," February 8, 1803, *Hamilton Papers*, 26:83; James Ross, speech of February 14, 1803, *Annals of Congress*, 7th Cong., 2nd sess., 86.

[46] Livingston to Madison, November 10, 1802, *Madison Papers (SSS)*, 4:110-11; Madison to Charles Pinckney, November 27, 1802, ibid., 147; Madison to Livingston and Monroe, March 2, 1803, ibid., 366. Italicized words were originally in code. It should be noted that both Livingston, in a subsequent letter, and Madison viewed the "wastepaper" language with some skepticism.

[47] Madison to Livingston, January 18, 1803, ibid., 259-60. Italicized words were originally in code.

[48] Madison to Livingston and Monroe, March 2, 1803, ibid., 377-78.

[49] Jefferson to Monroe, January 13, 1803, *Jefferson Writings*, 10:344; Jefferson to DuPont, February 1, 1803, ibid., 349.

50 Madison to Livingston, January 18, 1803, *Madison Papers (SSS)*, 4:260; Jefferson to Hugh Williamson, April 30, 1803, *Jefferson Writings*, 10:386; Jefferson to Bacon, April 30, 1803, *Jefferson Works*, 9:464; Jefferson to Williamson, April 30, 1803, *Jefferson Writings*, 10:386.

51 King to Madison, April 2, 1803, *Madison Papers (SSS)*, 4:475; Madison to Livingston and Monroe, April 18, 1803, ibid., 529. Italicized words were originally in code.

52 Jefferson to Meriwether Lewis, [June 20, 1803], Donald Jackson, ed., *The Letters of the Lewis and Clark Expedition with Related Documents, 1783-1854*, 2nd ed., 2 vols. (Urbana: University of Illinois Press, 1978), 1:61; Gallatin to Jefferson, April 13, 1803, *Gallatin Writings*, 1:120-22.

53 Livingston to Madison, December 10, 1801, *Madison Papers (SSS)*, 2:303; Livingston to Madison, September 1, 1802, ibid., 3:536. Italicized words were originally in code.

54 Livingston to Madison, November 2, 1802, ibid., 4:79.

55 Livingston to Madison, April 13, 1803, ibid., 512-13; Livingston to Madison, April 11, 1803, ibid., 500; Livingston to Madison, April 13, 1803, ibid., 513.

56 Livingston to Madison, April 13, 1803, ibid., 513 and 515.

57 Madison to Livingston and Monroe, March 2, 1803, ibid., 371.

58 Livingston to King, May 11, 1803, Edward Alexander Parsons, ed., *The Original Letters of Robert R. Livingston, 1801-1803; Written during his Negotiations of the Purchase of Louisiana* (New Orleans: Louisiana Historical Society, 1953), 64; Monroe to Madison, May 14, 1803, *Madison Papers (SSS)*, 4:610-11.

59 Livingston and Monroe to Madison, May 13, 1803, ibid., 601-3.

60 [Hamilton], "Purchase of Louisiana," July 5, 1803, *Hamilton Papers*, 26:129-31.

61 Ibid., 132-33.

62 Manasseh Cutler to unknown correspondent, October 31, 1803, William Parker Cutler and Julia Perkins Cutler, *Life, Journals and Correspondence of Rev. Manasseh Cutler, Ll.D.*, 2 vols. (Cincinnati, Ohio: Robert Clarke & Co., 1888), 2:140 (hereafter *Cutler Life*); William Plumer, diary entry of October 20, 1803, Everett Somerville Brown, ed., *William Plumer's Memorandum of Proceedings in the United States Senate, 1803-1807* (New York: The Macmillan Company, 1923), 6, 9 (hereafter *Plumer Memorandum*); "A Citizen," "Louisiana," *The Connecticut Courant* (Hartford), August 24, 1803; King to Christopher Gore, September 6, 1803, Charles R. King, ed., *The Life and Correspondence of Rufus King: Comprising His Letters, Private and Official, His Public Documents and His Speeches*, 6 vols. (New York: G. P. Putnam's Sons, 1894-1900), 4:303; "A Citizen," "Louisiana," *The Connecticut Courant* (Hartford), August 24, 1803.

63 Jefferson to Horatio Gates, July 11, 1803, *Jefferson Writings*, 10:402-3; Jefferson to Joseph Priestley, January 29, 1804, ibid., 446.

[64] Jefferson to Andrew Jackson, September 19, 1803, Sam B. Smith, et al., eds., *The Papers of Andrew Jackson*, 6 vols. to date (Knoxville: University of Tennessee Press, 1980—), 1:365 (hereafter *Jackson Papers*); Jefferson to John Dickinson, August 9, 1803, *Jefferson Works*, 10: 28.

[65] Gallatin to Jefferson, "Remarks on President's Message," [ca. October 1803], *Gallatin Writings*, 1:157; Madison to Monroe, July 30, 1803, *Madison Papers (SSS)*, 5:248.

[66] Smith to Jefferson, August 9, 1803, LC: Jefferson Papers; Claiborne to Jefferson, August 12, 1803, ibid.; Smith to Jefferson, August 9, 1803, ibid.; Clark to Madison, July 26, 1803, *Madison Papers (SSS)*, 5:226.

[67] Madison to Monroe, June 25, 1803, ibid., 118. Jefferson to George W. Erving, July 10, 1803, LC: Jefferson Papers. Italicized words were originally in code.

[68] Jefferson to Breckinridge, August 12, 1803, *Jefferson Writings*, 10:409-10; Jefferson to Priestley, January 29, 1804, ibid., 447.

[69] Jefferson to Priestley, January 29, 1804, ibid., 447; Jefferson, "Second Inaugural Address," March 4, 1805, James D. Richardson, comp., *A Compilation of the Messages and Papers of the Presidents, 1789-1897*, 10 vols. (Washington, D.C.: Government Printing Office, 1897-1899), 1:379 (hereafter *Messages and Papers*); Jefferson to Breckinridge, August 12, 1803, *Jefferson Writings*, 10:409.

[70] Lincoln to Jefferson, January 10, 1803, LC: Jefferson Papers; Gallatin to Jefferson, January 13, 1803, *Gallatin Writings*, 1:113-14; Jefferson to Gallatin, [January 13, 1803], ibid., 115.

[71] Jefferson, "Draft of an Amendment to the Constitution," [July 1803], *Jefferson Works*, 10:3; Jefferson to Dickinson, August 9, 1803, ibid., 29.

[72] Jefferson to Madison, August 25, 1803, *Jefferson Writings*, 10:414.

[73] Livingston to Jefferson, June 2, 1803, LC: Jefferson Papers; Jefferson to Madison, August 18, 1803, *Madison Papers (SSS)*, 5:323; Jefferson to Breckinridge, August 18, 1803, *Jefferson Works*, 10:8n. Italicized words were originally in code.

[74] Nicholas to Jefferson, September 3, 1803, LC: Jefferson Papers; Jefferson to Nicholas, September 7, 1803, *Jefferson Writings*, 10:419-20.

[75] Plumer, diary entry of October 20, 1803, *Plumer Memorandum*, 9; Samuel White, speech of November 2, 1803, *Annals of Congress*, 8th Cong., 1st sess., 33.

[76] Jefferson to DuPont, November 1, 1803, *Jefferson Writings*, 10:423.

[77] Livingston to Madison, May 20, 1803, *Madison Papers (SSS)*, 5:19.

[78] Jefferson to Madison, July 17, 1803, ibid., 191; Madison to Monroe, July 29, 1803, ibid., 240. Italicized words were originally in code.

79 Livingston and Monroe to Madison, June 7, 1803, ibid., 69; Gallatin to Jefferson, August 31, 1803, *Gallatin Writings*, 1:150; Jefferson to Breckinridge, August 12, 1803, *Jefferson Writings*, 10:408; Madison to Monroe, July 29, 1803, *Madison Papers (SSS)*, 5:243. Italicized words were originally in code.

80 Jefferson to Lincoln, August 30, 1803, *Jefferson Writings*, 10:417.

81 Jefferson to Horatio Gates, July 11, 1803, ibid, 402; Jefferson to DuPont, November 1, 1803, ibid., 423; Jefferson to Breckinridge, August 12, 1803, ibid., 410.

82 James Jackson, speech of February 17, 1804, as recorded in *Plumer Memorandum*, 143; White, speech of November 2, 1803, *Annals of Congress*, 8th Cong., 1st sess., 33-34; Jefferson to DeWitt Clinton, December 2, 1803, *Jefferson Works*, 10:55; Cocke's views as described by White, speech of November 2, 1803, *Annals of Congress*, 8th Cong., 1st sess., 34.

83 Jefferson to Breckinridge, August 12, 1803, *Jefferson Writings*, 10:410; Jefferson to Clinton, December 2, 1803, *Jefferson Works*, 10:55; Fisher Ames to Thomas Dwight, October 31, 1803, W. B. Allen, ed., *Works of Fisher Ames*, 2 vols. (Indianapolis, Ind.: Liberty Classics, 1983), 2: 1468-69.

84 Jefferson, "Special Message," October 21, 1803, *Messages and Papers*, 1:363; Cutler to Rev. Dr. Dana, November 30, 1803, *Cutler Life*, 2:148.

85 Monroe to Madison, September 17, 1803, *Madison Papers (SSS)*, 5:437; Jefferson to Madison, July 31, 1803, ibid., 255; Abraham Ellery to Hamilton, October 25, 1803, *Hamilton Papers*, 26: 165.

86 Jefferson to Breckinridge, August 12, 1803, *Jefferson Writings*, 10:410; Jefferson to Gallatin, [November 9, 1803], Clarence Edwin Carter, ed., *The Territorial Papers of the United States*, vol. 9, *The Territory of Orleans, 1803-1812* (Washington, D.C.: Government Printing Office, 1940), 100-101 (hereafter *Orleans Territorial Papers*).

87 Jefferson to Breckinridge, November 24, 1803, LC: Jefferson Papers; Jefferson, [draft bill], [ca. November 24, 1803], ibid. For Jefferson's draft of the government bill, see the text printed in James E. Seaton, "A Sudden Conceit: Jefferson and the Louisiana Government Bill of 1804," *Louisiana History* 9 (Spring 1968): 139-62.

88 Samuel White, speech of December 9, 1803, as recorded in *Plumer Memorandum*, 76; Adams, speech of December 5, 1803, as recorded in ibid., 73; Jefferson to Clinton, December 2, 1803, *Jefferson Works*, 10:55; Cocke, speech of January 16, 1804, as recorded in *Plumer Memorandum*, 108-9.

89 Jefferson to Jackson, September 19, 1803, *Jackson Papers*, 1:365; Jefferson to Priestley, January 29, 1804, *Jefferson Writings*, 10:447; Jefferson to the president, legislative council, Speaker of the House, and House of Representatives of the Indiana Territory, December 28, 1805, LC: Jefferson Papers; Jefferson to Madison, April 27, 1809, *Jefferson Writings*, 12:277. For the earliest surviving use of this phrase, see Jefferson to George Rogers Clark, December 25, 1780, in *Jefferson Papers*, 4:237–238.

90 Jefferson to DuPont, November 1, 1803, *Jefferson Writings*, 10:423.

91 Jefferson to Gallatin, [November 9, 1803], *Orleans Territorial Papers*, 100; Jefferson to John Holmes, April 22, 1820, *Jefferson Writings*, 15:249.

92 John Quincy Adams to John Adams, January 31, 1804, Adams Papers, microfilm edition, Massachusetts Historical Society, Boston, reel 403; "An Act for the Organization of Orleans Territory and the Louisiana District," [March 26, 1804], *Orleans Territorial Papers*, 209.

93 Claiborne to Cato West, December 20, 1803, printed in *National Intelligencer*, January 16, 1804, supplement; *National Intelligencer*, January 27, 1804; ibid., January 30, 1804; ibid., February 3, 1803.

94 Cutler to Dr. Torrey, January 26, 1804, *Cutler Life*, 2:161; Adams, diary entry, January 27, 1804, Charles Francis Adams, ed., *Memoirs of John Quincy Adams: Comprising Portions of His Diary from 1795 to 1848*, 12 vols. (Philadelphia: J. B. Lippincott & Co., 1874-1877), 1:293 (hereafter *Adams Memoirs*); Plumer, diary entry, January 27, 1804, *Plumer Memorandum*, 123; Adams, diary entry, January 31, 1804, *Adams Memoirs*, 1:293; Cutler to Mr. Poole, February 21, 1804, *Cutler Life*, 2:163.

95 "Plain Facts, No. V," *Washington Federalist*, February 3, 1804.

96 *National Intelligencer*, January 30, 1804; ibid., March 2, 1804; ibid., January 23, 1804; ibid., March 19, 1804.

97 Jefferson to Priestley, January 29, 1804, *Jefferson Writings*, 10:446-47.

98 "A Citizen," "Louisiana," *The Connecticut Courant* (Hartford), August 24, 1803.

Index

ABOUT THE MONTICELLO MONOGRAPH SERIES

This series, launched to commemorate the 250th anniversary of Jefferson's birth on April 13, 1993, consists of publications of enduring value on various aspects of Jefferson's diverse interests and legacy.

Also in print and currently available:

THOMAS JEFFERSON: A BRIEF BIOGRAPHY
by Dumas Malone

THE POLITICAL WRITINGS OF THOMAS JEFFERSON
edited by Merrill D. Peterson

SLAVERY AT MONTICELLO
by Lucia Stanton

JEFFERSON'S BOOKS
by Douglas L. Wilson

ARCHAEOLOGY AT MONTICELLO
by William M. Kelso

JEFFERSON AND RELIGION
by Eugene R. Sheridan

FREE SOME DAY: THE AFRICAN-AMERICAN FAMILIES OF MONTICELLO
by Lucia Stanton

JEFFERSON'S WEST: A JOURNEY WITH LEWIS AND CLARK
by James P. Ronda

THE LEVY FAMILY AND MONTICELLO 1834-1923:
SAVING THOMAS JEFFERSON'S HOUSE
by Melvin I. Urofsky

JEFFERSON AND SCIENCE
by Silvio A. Bedini

LETTERS FROM THE HEAD AND HEART: WRITINGS OF THOMAS JEFFERSON
by Andrew Burstein

Forthcoming:

JEFFERSON AND EDUCATION
by Jennings L. Wagoner